# HENRY FORD

# HENRY FORD
### An Interpretation

## SAMUEL S. MARQUIS
With an Introduction by David L. Lewis

Wayne State University Press  Detroit

11 10 09 08 07                          5 4 3 2 1

Library of Congress Cataloging-in-Publication Data
Marquis, Samuel S., 1866–1948.
Henry Ford : an interpretation / Samuel S. Marquis. — New ed.,
with an introduction by David L. Lewis.
     p. cm. — (Great Lakes books)
Originally published: Boston: Little, Brown, and Co., 1923.
Includes index.
ISBN-13: 978-0-8143-3367-9 (pbk. : alk. paper)
ISBN-10: 0-8143-3367-2 (pbk. : alk. paper)
1. Ford, Henry, 1863–1947. 2. Industrialists—United States—Biography.
3. Automobile industry and trade—United States—History.
I. Title.
CT275.F68M3 2007
973.91092—dc22
[B]
2007016887

∞ The paper used in this publication meets the minimum requirements of
the American National Standard for Information Sciences—Permanence of
Paper for Printed Library Materials, ANSI Z39.48-1984.

# CONTENTS

# CONTENTS

# INTRODUCTION

*David L. Lewis*

Seven books on Henry Ford were published in 1922 and 1923. Three were extremely eulogistic, one was a scathing attack, and another was reasonably objective, although inaccurate and cursory. Then there were Ford's *My Life and Work* and Samuel S. Marquis's *Henry Ford: An Interpretation.* In 1976 I described the latter as "one of the finest and most dispassionate character studies of Ford ever written." I think the same today.

Of the seven, only Ford's ghostwritten autobiography was a best-seller. Marquis's book would have been widely read had not the Ford organization been fairly successful in buying up copies and persuading book dealers not to sell it. A second printing was forestalled by Ford's purchase of book rights from Little, Brown, and Company in order to destroy the plates.

The Marquis book "became more or less a collector's item," William C. Richards states in his 1948 biography, *The Last Billionaire: Henry Ford*. "Copies stocked by the Detroit Public Library disappeared strangely and with such rapidity that there was much wondering as to whether [Fordmen] had withdrawn them and forgotten to bring them back. So many vanished in such a short time that the library retired remaining copies to its non-circulating shelves."

In his book Marquis writes sparingly of his personal life and pre-Ford career. Before proceeding, a few salient facts. He was born on a farm near Sharon, Ohio, on June 8, 1866, thus was three years younger than Henry Ford. A descendant of several generations of Episcopalian ministers, he was sent to Allegheny College in Meadville, Pennsylvania, to pursue ecclesiastical studies. Twice he was expelled because of "intense doubts" about religion. Subsequently reinstated, he graduated with a bachelor of arts degree and

# INTRODUCTION

honors in 1890. He then earned a bachelor of divinity degree at Cambridge Theology School in Massachusetts in 1893. Ordained as an Episcopalian priest, he served in churches in Woburn and Bridgewater, Massachusetts.

In 1899 Marquis was called to St. Joseph's Church in Detroit. Under his rectorship, the parish prospered, and he became one of the city's better known churchmen. In 1905 he was awarded a doctor of divinity degree by his alma mater, Allegheny. The next year he was assigned to St. Paul's parish, Detroit. As dean of St. Paul's he spearheaded the building of a handsome cathedral at 4800 Woodward Avenue. Meantime, in 1894 he was married to Gertrude Lee Snyder in Warren, Ohio. The couple had four children: Dorothy, born in 1895, Barbara Lee, 1897, Rogers Israel, 1901, and Gertrude Lee, 1907.

Marquis's duties at St. Paul's led to his exhaustion in 1915. His physician prescribed a year's leave of absence. The clergyman remonstrated, saying that a change of work would benefit him more than idleness. He became a volunteer in the two-year-old Sociological Department at Ford's Highland Park, Michigan, plant. A parishioner and friend, Henry Ford was elated, and in October 1915 invited the clergyman to join the department "and put Jesus Christ in my factory." In December, at the request of Ford's wife, Clara, Marquis accompanied Henry on the ill-fated voyage of the auto maker's "peace ship."

At the plant Marquis reported to the department's first head, John R. Lee. When Lee resigned in 1919 to join the Wills-Sainte Claire Company in Marysville, Michigan, Marquis took charge of the unit, subsequently renamed the Educational Department. Marquis's social work is fully discussed in his book and also in Alan Nevins's and Frank Ernest Hill's *Ford: Expansion and Challenge, 1915–1933*, which draws extensively on *An Interpretation*.

During Marquis's deanship at St. Paul's, the Marquises and Fords socialized. "Mother's and dad's and the Fords' relationship was very fine, friendly and simple," stated Barbara Marquis Carritte in 1952. "The Fords were very quiet and cordial people. They were satisfied to spend a quiet, yet stimulating, evening with mother and dad at any time that they could. They spent many evenings together." An assistant secretary in Henry Ford's office, Harold M. Cordell, similarly recalled that "The Marquises had entrée to the Fords' home and family circle." The Marquises were invited aboard the Fords' yacht and also accompanied the Fords and Mr. and Mrs. Thomas A. Edison on a chartered train that took them from Detroit to the inventor's hometown, Port Huron, Michigan. Marquis and Ford also footraced, Henry winning, Marquis handicapped by his forty-two-inch waistline. To Ford, Marquis was "Mark"; to Marquis, Ford was "Mr. Ford." The women had a cordial but formal relationship. In a lengthy February 5, 1917, letter, Clara addressed Gertrude as "Mrs. Marquis"; Clara presumably was "Mrs. Ford" to Gertrude.

The closeness of the Marquis/Ford relationship is suggested in a 1918 photo of the pair. Seated, the men's knees almost touch, and their elbows are two to three inches apart. In contrast is a posed 1915 picture of Ford and his principal partner, James Couzens. Mutually antagonistic, the pair, who shared no social life, are so far apart as to make the picture appear ludicrous.

Although many authors have mined Marquis's book, only Nevins, in his 1954 book, *Ford: The Times, the Man, the Company*, commented on the clergyman's personality, to wit: "A man of cheery temper, vigorous personality, and abounding energy, Marquis was keenly interested in economic conditions and the lot of the working man. . . . [He had] *a* genetic personality that drew conflicting elements into a unity, with the prophet's gift of preaching, with zeal and energy unbounded, and with vision of more than unusual power." Comparing Marquis and John R. Lee, Nevins observed, "Marquis was shorter, with a stocky figure and large head topped by curling dark gray hair; his Roman nose, close-set lips, and keen eyes gave an air of decision to his face, and altogether he looked more of a businessman than Lee. Both men were fluent of speech, and Marquis talked and wrote with a nice choice of phrase."

# INTRODUCTION

Marquis's appearance and manner of speech are mentioned in only two of the more than three hundred reminiscences of Henry Ford's employees and associates on file in the Benson Ford Research Center of The Henry Ford. Henry Ford's personal artist, Irving R. Bacon, a friend of the clergyman, saw in Marquis a "roguish Gritzner, monk-type countenance." Charles E. Sorensen, accused by Marquis (in the presence of Henry Ford) of interfering with Rouge plant production, observed, "It was a surprising accusation, but that did not take me aback half as much as the vigor of his language. I had always treated clergymen with deference. Many times in my life I have been called an s.o.b., but never before or after was I called one by a supposed man of God—in fact, that day I heard from Dean Marquis some words I'd never heard before."

Marquis backhandedly admitted a familiarity with strong language. Irritated by a Detroiter who criticized Edsel Ford's civilian status during World War I, he wrote, "Comment is unnecessary, and if couched in suitable language might not be considered fit to print."

Marquis operated unfettered at Highland Park. But when he attempted in the late teens to extend his authority to the burgeoning Rouge plant, he was thwarted by Sorensen and his subordinates. After appealing to Henry Ford for support, the clergyman was promised access to workers in the new factory. Meantime, Ford had assured Sorensen that Marquis's staff would not be allowed to interfere with production. Encouraged by his commitment from Ford, Marquis arranged for the founder, Sorensen, and himself to meet in Ford's Highland Park office. Marquis commented on the meeting in his book, and Sorensen offered his version in his 1956 volume, *My Forty Years with Ford*. "It was plain that [Marquis] had arranged this session with Mr. Ford, expecting to snow me under," Sorensen states:

When he started in on me, I wondered whether Mr. Ford was in accord with him or not. I had enough evidence to

make clear that he was interfering with
the operations of the plant, but the good
Dean was in no mood to listen. Then
he got as big a surprise as I had. He
was astonished to find that Mr. Ford
supported me in everything I had said
. . . and that both Mr. Ford and I were
set on his keeping his nose out of the
plant. Dean Marquis left the office in a
huff, and I never saw him again. A few
days later he sent in notice that he would
not carry on, and a great sigh of relief
went through the entire plant. Later on
. . . in a book, he treated Mr. Ford in as
ungrateful a way as did Harry Bennett,
who later headed an even more prying
and unpopular department in Ford Motor Company.

Disillusioned, disheartened, feeling be-
trayed, Marquis was devastated. Telling his
family "I don't know how long I can take
it, I think I'll get out," he resigned from
the company on January 25, 1921. "He often
said," Rogers Marquis remembered, "that he

hated like hell to think that it was Harry Bennett who would be his successor out there [the Rouge]."

Twenty-seven years later, an unidentified, undated Marquis obituary, likely published in a Detroit newspaper, reported that Marquis "walked away from an annual salary of $50,000." Mentioning the same figure, the *Chicago Daily Tribune* noted that "he returned to church work at less than $5,000 a year."

Henry Ford's personal artist, Irving R. Bacon, offered another explanation for Marquis's departure. His resignation, Bacon remarked, was precipitated by a speech made by the clergyman in Chicago in January 1921. At the time a sharp but brief recession gripped the country. Model T sales declined, and the heavily indebted Henry Ford was forced to suspend production, leaving him cash-strapped. Marquis, according to Bacon, "put the Boss on the spot. . . . Without authorization he stated that business conditions would make it impossible for the Ford Motor Company to pay their employees the annual bonus. That remark finished Dean Marquis; he was let out immediately. Despite the impending crisis, the Boss scraped together $7,500,000 in order to pay bonuses to his men."

In Clara Ford's mind, Marquis had resigned, and was the only high-level executive to do so among those who left the company between 1919 and 1921. "All the others were fired," she told Charles Voorhees, powerhouse engineer at the Fords' home. For a Ford executive, Marquis wrote, there were three certainties—"taxes, death, and discharge . . . he cometh up and is cut down like a flower."

Ford's duplicity angered Marquis and set the stage for the writing of his book. For more than a year he stewed over his friend's mishandling of his department and maltreatment of himself, other executives, and workers. Finally, he decided to write "a chapter" about Ford "to get [him] out of my mind in order that I might turn to other things. . . . But that chapter," he added, "slipped its tether and ran away with itself and with my thought and time." Marquis's son felt that *Detroit Free Press* editor Malcolm W. Bingay was a "moving spirit" behind the book. Surprisingly, Bingay does not mention the volume in his 1949 autobiography, *Of Me I Sing*. Of Marquis, he says only that the clergyman was "approached to do a sermon on what Jesus might have thought of municipal ownership of Detroit's streetcar system."

The preparation of *An Interpretation* created great family strain, as revealed in a taped interview of three Marquis children in 1952 by the Ford Archives. The interviewees were Rogers, Mrs. Barbara Carritte, and a Mrs. Johnson (first name unmentioned in the typescript, but likely Dorothy). The siblings agreed that their father's sense of betrayal prompted the book. "He was bitter in many spots," Barbara recalled. "He was very bitter."

"The whole family was in on the book," Rogers recalled, "and it pretty nearly split up the family." Marquis's wife was strongly opposed to the venture. "Mother was just terribly upset to think that he was writing the book," Mrs. Johnson remarked. "She did not want him to write it, and she did everything that she could to persuade him not to." "Mother edited it," Barbara added. "I can remember her saying, 'You cannot say that, you cannot say that. That reflects on you. It doesn't reflect on anybody else.' She was very careful of what got left in. She took the bitterness out." The siblings concurred that the finished manuscript was a "very sincere and honest effort on Dad's part to paint a portrait of the man as he saw him."

In the summer of 1922 Bacon visited Marquis in his "hideaway" (a cabin built by the family's own hands in rural Farmington, about a dozen miles northwest of Detroit). "He was in a rather vindictive mood toward the Boss," Bacon recalled, "and to get back at him he was writing a book entitled 'Henry Ford: An Interpretation.' Mrs. Marquis did not approve of this, and stated so, as he read passages from his manuscript to me. I thought too he was making a great mistake and should have been grateful to Mr. Ford for all that he had done for him and the $35,000 yearly salary which he had been drawing for years."

Shortly after the visit, Bacon, while filming yacht races, encountered Ford on the judges' stand. "There he was, togged out in a yachting outfit, cap and all," Bacon stated. "In greeting him, I mentioned having seen Marquis and quoted a passage from his manuscript. His only comment was, 'Poor fellow.'" Ford dismissed the book, according to William C. Richards, by saying that it was "about the parson, not me."

Marquis was the first Ford intimate to criticize the industrialist in print. Aware that he was treading on thin ice, Marquis recalled that Ford had told him that "the best friend one has is the man who tells him the truth." Hopefully, the clergyman remarked, "[he] will receive the critical portion of these pages in the same spirit." Ford emphatically did not.

"Bang! Zip!" Barbara recalled. "There was no more relationship between father and mother and Mr. and Mrs. Ford after the book was published. Oh, Dad was terribly upset. . . . Mother told me that there were a number of years that Mr. Ford was very hurt and very angry at Dad. Then Dad was taken to the Ford Hospital, and one day Mr. Ford came in to see him. . . . Anyway they patched it up to a little beyond the nodding acquaintance." Mrs. Marquis, however, would never be spoken to again by Henry and Clara. "Mrs. Ford never forgot the book," Rogers commented.

"But prior to her death I saw her two or three times out at Holiday House and at Girls' Friendly Association, and spoke to her. She was very pleasant to me." Barbara also recalled that Mrs. Ford was "always very friendly" toward her. "I was working in the Admitting Department at the Ford Hospital after it was taken back from the government. She used to come to the Ford Hospital and into my office and sit and chat. She was a very simple, nice, quiet person."

*An Interpretation* has nineteen chapters, ranging in length from three to thirteen pages. "The chapters are not strung together on any logical or chronological basis," the author explains. "They are as beads loose in a box, and you are at liberty to take them and examine them in any order you wish." Readers thus may be tempted to delve first into chapters with such intriguing titles as "The Ford Halo," "Lights," "Shadows," "An Elusive Personality," "The Art of Self-Advertising," "Mental Traits and Characteristics," "Behind a Chinese Wall," and "The Ford Executive Scrap Heap."

Two chapters are devoted to Henry Ford's son, Edsel. Some Ford executives were mentioned by name; others were not. Among those named were John R. Lee, business manager and stockholder James Couzens, sales manager Norval A. Hawkins, and advertising manager Charles A. "Daddy" Brownell. Unnamed but readily identifiable to students of Ford history were Ford's executive secretary Ernest G. Liebold and manufacturing men Sorensen, P. E. Martin, and William C. Klann.

Marquis does not overstate his understanding of Ford. "In spite of a long and fairly intimate acquaintance with him," he writes, "I have not one mental picture of him . . .

of which I can say, 'This is as he is.'. . .
There are in him lights so high and shadows
so deep that I cannot get the whole of him
in proper focus. . . . No satisfactory portrait
of him ever will be made." Sorensen, Ford's
top manufacturing executive, was more sure
of himself. "In many ways," he claims in his
1956 autobiography, *My Forty Years with
Ford*, "I knew him better than did members
of his family." Similarly, the back cover of
Harry Bennett's book, *We Never Called Him
Henry*, declares that the Ford aide/crony
"was the closest human to Henry Ford."

As for myself, in 1976 I wrote, "Since 1952
I have read and thought a great deal about
Henry Ford, published more than a million
words about him, exclusive of this book [*The
Public Image of Henry Ford*], and visited all
of his familiar haunts. I probably know more
about Ford's life and work than any other
writer. But I cannot say that I have com-
pletely sorted him out nor am I sure that I
shall ever fully understand him." Thirty-one
years and millions of words later, I feel the
same. That Ford remains a puzzle partially

explains the constant stream of literature about him.

Marquis, along with being highly observant, was erudite and philosophic. Often comparing Ford and his associates with others, he wrote, "Ford and the 'Grand Llama of Thibet' were equally inaccessible," and Ford and Lloyd George "lost faith with their early idealism"; "Lazarus," he noted, "would not lie unnoticed very long at the gate of Henry Ford. . . . Something would be done to put him on his feet, something more than giving him a crumb or a coin"; "Joseph," he added, "lived to see his dream come true and to receive the homage of the men who ridiculed and hated him. Will Henry Ford pardon me for discovering this striking resemblance between himself and a man of a race in which he seems able to see so few virtues and so many faults?" Of the brusque Liebold, assigned to block access to Ford, he wrote, "A Chesterfield might suggest that which here and there would add grace and charm to the manner in which his job is handled but he certainly could do nothing to raise the present standard of efficiency."

The author's phraseology also delights, for example, "Ford has in him the making of a great man, the parts lying about in more or less disorder. If only Henry Ford were properly assembled!"; "The isolation of Henry Ford's mind is about as near perfect as it is possible to make it"; "The spotlight cannot be shifted fast enough to keep him [Ford] out of it"; "I think St. Peter will pass Mr. Ford at the gate, but following that I fear that he and Abraham will have to iron out some misunderstandings."

"You cannot say that it is a matter of luck that a man's [Ford's] boat is floated by the rising tide, if he has carefully calculated the time the tide comes in and has built his boat where it would be caught and carried out to sea"; "Every time any one handed John R. Lee a bouquet for his bigness of heart he tossed it over to Henry, and when there was no one around explained to him what it was all about. And Henry kept the flowers."

In 1954 Roger Burlingame, author of *Henry Ford*, the best brief biography of the magnate, expressed the wish that Marquis "had been a better writer." I believe that he wrote exceedingly well.

*An Interpretation* appeared in the midst of a 1923 "Ford-for-President" boomlet, as reflected in the handful of reviews in the Samuel Simpson Marquis papers in the Cranbrook Archives, Bloomfield Hills, Michigan. There are no reviews of the book in the press scrapbooks at the Benson Ford Research Center, even though the 167 oversized albums contain editorials and news and feature stories on nearly all aspects of Henry Ford's life from 1911 onward. It seems as if the compilers were instructed to ignore the book, or thought it prudent to do so.

All of the reviews are favorable. An undated 1923 *Boston Herald* account, titled "The Paradox of Henry Ford," describes the book as "most entertaining and informative." It also expresses regret that Marquis "does not mention some of the matters which would be exceedingly interesting to many people, such as Ford's motive and objective in his treatment of the Jewish question." Actually,

# INTRODUCTION

*An Interpretation* briefly mentions Ford's anti-Semitism, while grossly shortchanging the subject.

An undated 1923 review by Frederic F. Van de Water in an unidentified publication observes that *An Interpretation* "is not in the least the sort of volume one might expect from a man who was dean of St. Paul's Cathedral, Detroit . . . [and] much of it could never be used as [presidential] campaign material by Ford boosters." "Despite its accusatory tone," Van de Water adds, "the book as a whole carries with it an air of fairness, of sympathy, of compassion. Marquis does not assail. He does not point out weaknesses with a sense of triumph. He paints the dreamer whose feet do not rest on an enduring foundation and of a shy, moody billionaire who loves birds."

A *New York Times* review from April 29, 1923, states:

Close observation of Ford's characteristics, coupled with an evidently independent mind and a keen psychological interest in human nature has enabled the author *to* write *in the first* place an exceedingly entertaining book and, in the second, the most truthfully illuminating discussion of the Ford mind and heart that has yet been made. He aims always to be absolutely just and he tries to get down behind some of the things Ford has done to arouse both praise and blame and to find out and make clear why he did them. The result is not by any means a full portrait—nobody probably knows Henry Ford well enough to make that—but some sketchy outlines that preserve certain gracious and powerful features and do not attempt to conceal any of the warts or harsh lines or lack of symmetry. It reveals, also what to many will be a surprise, that in the maker of the car of world-wide fame dwells an extraordinarily interesting, puzzling, and complex nature.

The *Times*'s reviewer also regretted that Marquis "does not mention some of the matters which would be of exceeding interest to many people, such as Ford's motive and objective in his treatment of the Jewish question."

The lengthiest of the reviews, a three-and-half-page essay titled "Why Henry Ford Should Not Be President," appeared in the May 30, 1923, issue of the *Nation*. Describing Marquis as Ford's "Boswell," editor Oswald Garrison Villard comments, "The book is of especial significance at this [politically charged] time, and is remarkable in itself for its extraordinary detachment and its refreshing honesty, so rare in biographies of this type. Should Mr. Ford be nominated for the Presidency this book ought to be placed in the hands of every voter. For on almost every page are convincing reasons why he should not be sent to the White House."

Fearful of Ford's possible candidacy, Villard observed, "The best-informed political observers say that if Ford is nominated on the Democratic ticket he will sweep the country. That is why many of them think that even without the endorsement of either of the major parties he can run on a third ticket and be elected. If either contingency should come to pass the result would be disastrous to Henry Ford and to the country." Marquis felt the same. He granted, however, that the auto king, "as President . . . would be able to give us a very economical administration, for a Cabinet and Congress would be entirely superfluous if he were in the White House."

Had Ford been a presidential candidate, Marquis's book likely would have been more widely circulated, Ford's suppressive efforts notwithstanding. It could have influenced the 1924 primaries and general election. In any event, the Ford boomlet fizzled after Clara declared she would have none of it. Henry, who valued domestic peace at any price, bowed to her dictate.

One publisher's advertisement of *An Interpretation* is filed in Cranbrook's Marquis papers. A small ad titled "Henry Ford's Fitness for the Presidency," in an unidentified publication, asserts that the book "is by one who knows Ford best of all. . . . This X-ray of the world's greatest automobile manufacturer is generous, but it has moments of remorseless intellectual surgery."

# INTRODUCTION

Several authors have evaluated Marquis's book. Nevins described it as a "critical, revealing portrait." Burlingame remarked, "of the books that both praise and blame, two are outstanding. These are Samuel S. Marquis's *Henry Ford: An Interpretation* . . . and William C. Richards's *The Last Billionaire: Henry Ford*. "Marquis," he added "knew Ford more intimately, probably, than anyone outside his immediate family." William A. Simonds's 1943 book, *Henry Ford: His Life, His Work, His Genius*, mentions Marquis five times. But being a Ford employee, Simonds judged neither the clergyman nor his book. Douglas Brinkley, in his 2003 book, *Wheels for the World: Henry Ford, His Company, and a Century of Progress, 1903–2003*, observed that "Marquis was a good writer who made for a bad enemy; his book was scathing in its description of Henry Ford's fading commitment to anything other than making money."

I regard *An Interpretation* as being straightforward, evenhanded, and lucid. Moreover, Marquis, who did not invent conversations, was surely better qualified than anyone else to interpret Henry Ford in his prime inasmuch he had unparalleled business *and* social familiarity with his subject. Also, he was observant, perceptive, and thoughtful.

If Marquis's early drafts were strident, the finished product is soft-edged, thanks, one presumes, to his wife's admonitions and editing. The book, however, seems less gentle as the writing moves beyond chapters 11 and 13, "The Ford Executive Scrap Heap" and "Industrial Scavengers," respectively. Even so, the author does not exaggerate, rant, or preach. He obviously found the truth big enough. As for appearance, the book featured twelve-point type, wide margins, and nonslick pages, all comforting to an octogenarian reader such as myself.

I first read *An Interpretation* in 1953, and began rereading it the evening of July 21, 2006. The following morning I wrote, "Read Marquis book until 10:30 [usual bedtime]. Couldn't sleep, thinking about it. Got up [exceptional for me] at 12:30 to resume reading.

Finished it at 2:15. Took 15 pages of notes. Wished there were more to read, especially a chapter on HF's homespun opinions on Jews and African-Americans."

The book's index is well done. One presumes that the Marquises prepared it, or at least closely supervised its preparation. The "Ford, Henry" entry, chock-full of subentries, covers two and a half pages, the "Marquis" entry one and a half pages. By way of contrast, the "Couzens, James" entry in Nevins's first Ford volume is followed by 83 *unbroken* page numbers. Might as well look for a needle in a haystack. Forget it.

After leaving Ford in 1921 Marquis again served as rector of St. Joseph's. Three years later, at the invitation of wealthy publisher George G. Booth, he moved to Bloomfield Hills, Michigan, to assist in the establishment of a new parish, Christ Church Cranbrook. As missionary-in-charge, he conducted services in the Meeting House (now Brookside School) and helped to supervise the completion of subsequent parish structures.

When Christ Church Cranbrook parish was

officially established in 1927, Marquis was appointed director, a capacity in which he served until 1938. He also was instrumental in founding Cranbrook School for Boys and served as a trustee from 1926 to 1939. In 1940 a dormitory, Marquis Hall, was dedicated in his honor. Attending the ceremony were the student body, school officials, the Episcopal bishop of Michigan, and benefactors Mr. and Mrs. Booth. A bronze tablet, created by a 1940 Cranbrook graduate, was placed on the west wall of the hall near the south entrance. It reads:

Marquis Hall
A.D.—1927
In Honor of The Rev. S.S. Marquis, D.D.
Rector Christ Church Cranbrook
1927–1938

Photographed standing beside the marker, the seventy-four-year-old Marquis was supported by a cane, perhaps two canes (the photo is unclear in this regard). "Ill health forced Dr. Marquis to retire," states a 1940 Cranbrook document that fails to mention a retirement date. In perhaps his last public photograph, Marquis stood caneless among three other founders of the Henry Ford Trade School on July 1, 1946.

Mrs. Marquis died on October 26, 1940. Her husband succumbed at eighty-two on June 21, 1948, "after a long illness" (often a euphemism for cancer), reported the *Chicago Daily Tribune*. In the one other obituary in Cranbrook's Marquis papers, an unidentified Detroit newspaper states, "Thousands of Detroiters felt their loss today in the death of a white-haired friend who believed in a religion of social reform and would not preach 'a paradise hereafter as reward for hell on earth.'" Funeral services for Dr. Marquis were held in Christ Church Cranbrook. He and his wife are buried in Greenwood Cemetery, Birmingham, Michigan.

Marquis's most important legacy is his book. Subsequent to its publication, the clergyman did not publicly discuss either his tome or Henry Ford. Perhaps he was not asked to do so, or if asked, declined. Had he lived three years longer, the Oral History Section of the

# INTRODUCTION

Ford Archives, established in 1951, surely would have sought him out. In any event, he bequeathed *Henry Ford: An Interpretation*, and Wayne State University Press deserves the highest commendation for reprinting it as part of its Great Lakes Books Series. Other books in the series include reprints of Harry Barnard's 1958 *Independent Man: The Life of Senator James Couzens* and Charles E. Sorensen's autobiography *My Forty Years with Ford*.

In 1998 the Henry Ford Museum and Greenfield Village (now units of The Henry Ford) named seven adult "Books to Read About Henry Ford." They were by Allan Nevins and Frank Ernest Hill, one each by Peter Collier/David Horowitz, Jeanine Head/William S. Pretzel, Robert Lacey, and myself. Marquis's book should have been included.

Marquis is one of thirty-seven Fordmen to whom a chapter is devoted in Ford R. Bryan's 1993 book, *Henry's Lieutenants*. He is one of five persons, Henry Ford among them, portrayed on the book's jacket.

Marquis's papers are deposited in the

# INTRODUCTION

Cranbrook Archives and the Benson Ford Research Center (former Ford Archives). The Cranbrook papers were donated by Rogers Marquis and Barbara Marquis Carritte in 1983 and 1986, respectively.

Tangible monuments to Marquis's memory are Marquis Hall and St. Paul's Cathedral, in which last rites were conducted for Edsel, Henry, and Clara Ford in 1943, 1947, and 1950, respectively.

Summing up Henry Ford, Marquis remarked, "As for halos [vs. horns], they may be left to the biting frosts of time. History, in spite of Mr. Ford's gibes at her, will ultimately put him in the niche in which he belongs, with or without a halo according to his deserts." Amen.

# HENRY FORD
## AN INTERPRETATION

## INTRODUCTION

THIS book is all about Henry Ford, so far as it goes, but it is not the story of his life, not a record of events beginning with his birth and brought down to the present hour. The Ford chronicles make interesting reading, but they have been done in reel and rime and reams of prose. It yet remains to set them to music, and one of these days we may have a Ford symphony beginning with the faint flute notes of an infant's cry, swelling into the tremulous tragic tones of the strings, expressive of early struggles, and bursting finally into a veritable din with crash of cymbals, roll of drums and flare of trumpets, giving a tone picture of the roar of Ford factories and the rumble of the chariot wheels of success, and ending—but I leave that to the musicians.

# INTRODUCTION

Those who like to do that kind of thing may set down in order the events of Mr. Ford's life — the stories of boyhood days, the struggles of early years, and the achievements of later life. Personally, I am more interested in the operations of that mental machine which he carries under his hat than in all that other machinery of iron and steel massed under the roofs of those vast buildings in Highland Park and on the banks of the Rouge. I know of no study more absorbing than the Ford psychology, and I find myself turning to it in my leisure hours as to a form of pleasure and recreation. One finds so many things in it that are not in the books.

So, what follows, is not the life of Henry Ford, but an attempt at an interpretation of him in a series of brief chapters, or essays, which are not strung together on any logical or chronological string. They are as beads loose in a box, and you are at liberty to take them up and examine them in any order you please.

I have not written with the public in mind but rather because the fascinating character of the study I was pursuing made it necessary to get it out of my mind in order that I might turn to other things. I have not worked as at a task, but as at an absorbingly interesting as well as a more or less entertaining pastime, as one would work at a psychological puzzle such as the unusual mind and baffling personality of Henry Ford presents. As a matter of fact, what follows was meant to be a brief introductory chapter to a book of another sort. But that first chapter slipped its tether and ran away with itself and with my thought and time. It seemed endowed with a sort of amœbous power to divide and subdivide itself until, instead of a brief introductory chapter to another book, it became a little book in itself.

So there you have what this book is all about, what it aims to be, and how it happened to be just what it is.

# CHAPTER I

I HAVE known Henry Ford for twenty years. For a time he was my parishioner, and then for a time I was his employee.

Given freedom to create a man will reveal himself in what he produces — the painter in his picture, the sculptor in his marble, the writer in his book, the musician in his composition, and the mechanic in his machine. The Ford car is Henry Ford done in steel, and other things. Not a thing of art and beauty, but of utility and strength — the super-strength, power and endurance in engine and chassis, but somewhat ephemeral in its upper works. With top torn, body dented, upholstery gone, fenders rattling, and curtains flapping in the wind, you admire the old thing and speak softly and affectionately of it, because under the little hood the engine — occasionally

4

on four, sometimes on three, frequently on two, and now and then on one — keeps rhythmically chugging along, keeps going when by all the laws of internal combustible things it ought to stop and with one weary expiring gasp fall to pieces and mingle with the mire its few remaining grains of rust. But it keeps going, just as he keeps going contrary to all the laws of labor, commerce and high finance.

Some years ago I sat in the office of a Ford executive, discussing with him a certain thing the " chief " had ordered done. " It's a fool thing, an impossible thing," said the executive, " but he has accomplished so many impossible things that I have learned to defer judgment and wait the outcome. Take the Ford engine, for example; according to all the laws of mechanics the damned thing ought not to run, but it does."

As in the Ford engine, so in Henry Ford there are things that by all the laws of ordinary and industrial life should " queer " him, put him out of the running, but he keeps going.

He is an extraordinary man, a personality in the sense that he is different from other people, quite different, for that matter, from what he is popularly supposed to be.

But however unlike the rest of us Henry Ford may be in some respects, he falls under the classification of ordinary mortals in this: he is not satisfied with what he has and is.

He is one of the richest men on earth. He is the most widely known man in the industrial world. But with these things he is not content. He has other ambitions. For example, he not only has the willingness, but has shown a rather strong desire to assume national political responsibilities. And on one occasion he voluntarily took upon himself the task of settling the problems of a world at war. His ability to do in other than the industrial sphere may be commensurate with his will, but his efforts in other directions have not been such as to inspire confidence.

It is not only the absence of certain qualifications, but the presence of others that make us doubt his fitness for the field of politics. If our Government were an absolute monarchy, a one-man affair, Henry Ford would be the logical man for the throne. As President, and he seems to have aspirations in that direction, he would be able to give us a very economical administration, for a Cabinet and Congress would be entirely superfluous if he were in the White House. The chances are that he would run the Government, or try to do so, as he runs his industry, having had experience along no other lines. The Ford organization would be transferred to Washington. That would not be so difficult a matter as it might appear to the uninitiated. It could be accomplished in a single section of a Pullman car, with one in the upper and two in the lower berth. I agree with Mr. Edison, who was recently reported as saying of Mr. Ford, " He is a remarkable man in one sense, and in another he is not. I would not vote for him for President, but as a director of manufacturing or industrial enterprises I'd vote for him — twice."

But I doubt if the spark of political ambition in him ever would have burst into flame had it been left to itself. There are those near him, however, who never cease to blow upon it and fan it, being themselves ambitious to sit in the light of the political fire which by chance may be kindled in this way. They seem to entertain no doubt of their ability to run any office for him from that of the Presidency down.

But Henry Ford has left upon me the impression that his chief ambition is to be known as a thinker of an original kind. He has the not uncommon conviction among mortals that he has a real message for the world, a real service to render mankind.

" I want to live a life," he said to me some years ago when we were returning from Europe after the Peace Ship fiasco. " Money means nothing to me — neither the making of it nor the use of it, so far as I am personally concerned. I am in a peculiar position. No one can give me anything. There is nothing I want that I cannot have. But I do not want the things money can buy. I want to live a life, to make the world a little better for having lived in it. The trouble with people is that they do not think. I want to do things and say things that will make them think."

In my opinion he could realize his supreme ambition if he were to follow the example of a good shoemaker and stick to his last, that is, to the human and production problems in industry, and leave national, international and racial problems alone. It is human to grow weary of achievement in one direction. Like Alexander, we tearfully long for adventures in other worlds instead of trying to bring a little nearer to perfection the world we have conquered.

For many years Mr. Ford shunned the public gaze, refused to see reporters, modestly begged to be kept out of print; and then suddenly faced about, hired a publicity agent, jumped into the front page of every newspaper in the country, bought and paid for space in which he advertised what were supposed to be his own ideas (although he admitted in the *Chicago Tribune* trial that he had not even read much that had been put out under his own name) and later bought a weekly publication and began to run "his own page." I think he would rather be the maker of public opinion than the manufacturer of a million automobiles a year, which only goes to show that in spite of the fact that he sticks out his tongue at history, he would nevertheless not object to making a little of it himself.

This laudable ambition to serve the world, and, in some degree, to mold its thought, has very naturally aroused in men the desire to know more intimately this man who volunteers to take the part of Moses — he doesn't put it just this way — in a world-exodus into a new era of peace and prosperity. Having made himself a world figure, or persisting in being reckoned as one, the world insists, and properly so, on knowing all there is to know about him. It is the price every man must pay for aspiring to such an exalted position.

" Tell me now, in confidence, is Henry Ford as great a man as the people generally believe him to be? Is he the brains of the organization which bears his name? Is its success due to him, or to the men he has gathered about him? Is he anything more than a mechanical genius? Is it true that he cannot read and write? Is he a financier? Does he keep in touch with the details of his business? Is he a hard worker? Is he sincere, or a self-advertiser?" These are some of the questions people keep asking you if you chance to have a fairly intimate acquaintance with Henry Ford.

The " tell me now in confidence " phrase is significant. It means that the questioner has a lurking suspicion that the popular idol of Dearborn is not all gold. There must be some clay in his make-up. It would be a great satisfaction to have a well authenticated sample of the clay.

Not long ago I delivered an address on the Ford way of handling labor. The membership of the organization to which I was speaking was composed chiefly of working men. The president of the club introduced me and closed his remarks by saying, " Now that you are no longer in the employ of Henry Ford, tell us the truth about him." The same lurking suspicion. If only the truth were told! If only those who know him intimately would tell all they knew, — well, if it did not take the halo from his head it might, at least, give it a jocular slant.

Speaking of halos, I am reminded of a row of saints which occupied the niches above the altar in a certain theological seminary. They were made of marble, and each had upon his head a halo, also of marble, and resembling nothing so much as a large dinner plate. Winter had a disastrous effect upon these halos. The frost cracked them and they fell off. A sudden drop in temperature during the night meant that one or more of those blessed saints would be minus a nimbus in the morning.

There are those who would like to see what effect a frost would have on the halo of Henry Ford. They want to know the worst, not to "have it over," but to help "put it over." If there be such among my readers they are going to be more or less disappointed. I was accused not long ago by a prominent labor leader of being more responsible than any other one man for creating the Ford halo. He thought I ought to try to take it off. But why waste one's time? Once a halo is on, the wearer of it is the only one who can take it off. If he proves himself worthy, the halo sticks; if otherwise, the halo fades of itself. For the present, I am interested neither in taking the Ford halo off, nor in holding it on.

The truth is, as everybody knows, there is

some clay in every popular idol. There is some in Henry Ford.

It would be possible to write a book made up entirely of adverse criticism of both himself and his company, every word of which would be true, and yet the book on the whole would be utterly false and misleading, as false and misleading as one of unstinted praise.

There are things that are laudable in both the man and his company, and there are things in both which it is a pity are there. I shall endeavor to state the truth in a frank and friendly manner. It may be that such publicity will tend to eliminate some of the things which cause us to mingle regret with our admiration.

On the return journey from Europe above referred to I found it necessary to make a very frank criticism of certain ideas advanced by Mr. Ford. It was to the effect that if he stuck to the things he knew, and let those alone about which his training had not qualified him to venture an opinion, he would avoid placing himself in a foolish position. The criticism stuck. I have heard him refer to it many times since. The last time he mentioned the matter in my presence he added, " And I have come to the conclusion that the best friend one has is the man who tells him the truth." I hope he will receive the critical portion of these pages in the same spirit. They are meant to help, for I would like to see that halo stick.

But as for halos, — they may be left to the biting frosts of time. History, in spite of Mr. Ford's gibes at her, will ultimately put him in the niche in which he belongs, with or without a halo according to his deserts.

# CHAPTER II

THE ordinary mortal is content to hitch his wagon to a star. This is a sport too tame for Henry Ford. He prefers to hang on to the tail of a comet. It is less conventional, more spectacular and furnishes more thrills.

Mr. Ford seems to love sensations, to live in them and to be everlastingly creating them, jumping from one to another. And many of his sensational acts and utterances are so clever that the world looks on with something more than amusement. In spite of the fact that he has come near making a clown of himself on more than one occasion, the audience, for the most part, continues to watch him with wonder and admiration. He has been right so many times in industrial matters, done so many admirable and worth-while things, that we are inclined to forget the times he has been wrong or foolish.

15

# HENRY FORD

I suppose that an acrobat with a net under him takes risks that he would not take if he were looking down on the bare hard earth. In like manner, I suppose, the fact that one has under him several hundred millions to fall back on renders him more or less indifferent to a tumble. He can afford to try stunts he would otherwise hesitate to undertake. But whatever the reason, Henry Ford appears to be drawn to the limelight as a moth to a candle. If he comes out slightly singed, as in the case of the Peace Ship and the *Tribune* trial, he nevertheless comes gayly and boldly back to flutter around a Semitic or other candle. One cannot but marvel at the continuance of the public's patience, interest and faith.

There is a popular interest in Henry Ford which is not difficult of explanation. The world's chief interest is, and always has been, in successful men. It does not matter much in what field their achievement lies, so long as they have achieved. Captain Kidd, Jesse James, Babe Ruth, Ty Cobb, Sullivan, Dempsey, Samson, Goliath of Gath, Napoleon, Washington, Grant, Foch, Lincoln, Homer,

Shakespeare, Angelo, Wagner, Charlie Chaplin, Rockefeller, Morgan, Schwab, Carnegie, Edison, Ford — pirates, outlaws, four-base hitters, prize fighters, soldiers, statesmen, writers, painters, composers, movie stars, financiers, inventors — we are interested in them, if only they are a success. And we want to know all there is to know about them.

Henry Ford is among the top-notchers in the field of achievement along industrial lines. He is in the class of highly successful men, and he shares in the interest which the world gives to this class as a whole.

But more of popular interest attaches to Mr. Ford than to any other man of his class. He is the most widely known, the most talked-of, and — among the masses — the most popular man in private life to-day, and has been for the past ten years. How account for it?

It is said of him that he is always doing sensational things — some wise, some foolish; that he is the best self-advertiser of the age; that the spotlight cannot be shifted fast enough to keep him out of it. Henry Ford does do sensational things. In addition to that he frequently makes sensational attempts to do things he is unable to do. And from the self-advertising point of view, a sensational attempt is almost always as valuable for immediate purposes as a sensational achievement. The man who proposes to ride Niagara Falls in a barrel has several weeks before the event in which to enjoy the publicity that will be given him, and to exhibit the barrel for a consideration. If he survives his sensational undertaking, the barrel will be of still greater value to him. If he should not chance to come up after his spectacular plunge, and it was a taste of notoriety he craved, he had what he wanted for a brief time and, presumably, died happy.

Of course, the man who insists on standing all the time in the calcium ray must expect to be put under the X-ray. And the shadows cast by these two rays are quite different.

The man who attempts to do sensational things entirely out of his sphere and beyond his power will, in time, wear down the public's confidence in his judgment. Henry Ford is not so widely admired as he once was. Grant that a man is sincere in trying to do what he is not fitted to do, that will not prevent men mingling pity with their admiration. And pity, when too frequently aroused, is in danger of turning into a mild contempt.

Henry Ford made a spectacular attempt to end the World War. The Peace Ship brought a flood of publicity — fame or notoriety — just as one looks at it. I questioned his judgment at the time, but not his motive. And I still believe his motive back of that undertaking was a laudable one. If all the facts were known, I think it would be admitted that he did not deserve the ridicule that was heaped upon him. To me, during the early months of the war, he was a pathetic and much misunderstood figure. I endeavored to persuade him to abandon the Peace Ship project, or at least to modify his plans. His old friend, Mr. William Livingstone, and myself spent the most of the night before the expedition sailed trying to prevail upon him to abandon it. It was no use. His reply to me was, " It is right, is it not, to try to stop war? " To that I could only answer, " Yes." " Well," he would go on, " you have told me that what is right cannot fail." And the answer to that, that right things attempted in the wrong way had no assurance of success, had no effect. He was following what he calls a "hunch," and when he gets a " hunch " he generally goes through with it, be it wise or foolish, right or wrong.

But to the credit of Henry Ford it must be said that he has done sensational things of a higher and saner order. He has done a number of things in industry because he thought them right and just, and the world has labeled them sensational. But it was not the thing in itself that was sensational, but the fact that he had the courage to do it. It ought not to be counted a sensational thing that a man loves his wife, but in a community where it is supposed no man cares for his wife, it might create more or less of a sensation to find one who does. And surely such a man should not be charged with bidding for notoriety. Henry Ford has done many things in the handling of labor which, if all employers were doing by labor as they should, would not be counted sensational at all.

# THE ART OF SELF-ADVERTISING

In 1914 Mr. Ford agreed with Mr. Couzens that, in view of the earnings of the company, the men in their employ should be given an increase in pay. Mr. Couzens dared him to make the minimum pay five dollars a day, and Mr. Ford agreed. It was nothing more than a company in the financial position the Ford company was then in should do. Few, however, do it. Hence the sensation when Henry Ford did it.

He increases wages and at the same time reduces the cost of the car. Sensational! But why should it be considered a sensational thing to give the customer some of the benefits which the increasing prosperity of a company makes it possible to bestow? Why — except that few do it? Shrewd business? Good advertising? Certainly, it is all that, and more. There can be no greater shrewdness in business than to follow the laws of honest and just dealing, provided you expect to remain any length of time in business.

I went to the Ford Motor Company with the conviction that it pays in industry in the long run to do the thing that is right, just and humane. I left the company with that conviction more firmly fixed in my mind than ever. This universe is one, and the laws in one sphere of life are not in conflict with those of another. What is wrong out of business cannot be right within it.

There was a time when I smiled skeptically at the Old Testament teaching that the reward of righteousness is milk and honey and the recompense of the God-fearing man is sheep and camels. It did not seem to me, so far as my observation went, to work out that way. But I have lived long enough to see that it does work out that way in the end.

Wealth is created by society, and belongs to and is meant to be enjoyed by society. The tendency is always in the direction of the redistribution of wealth unjustly acquired and held as an individual possession. In the heart of every selfishly made and selfishly controlled fortune there is concealed the seed of a social and industrial revolution. It may be an ugly fact to face, but it is a fact nevertheless, borne out by the history of centuries. The day of reckoning may be postponed, but it comes.

Dimly society is beginning to see this, and slowly, but surely, the time is coming — in fact, it is now here — when individuals will be permitted to possess great wealth only on the condition that they regard themselves as the stewards of it, and not owners.

It pays to give all one can out of a business and still keep a safe margin on which to continue operations. Because Henry Ford has done this — and it must be conceded that he has done it — he is about the only man in this country to-day of great wealth of whom the masses are not critical and envious, and to whom they would willingly entrust still greater wealth. Not only would they give him Muscle Shoals, but they would throw in the mines and railroads of the country. He has demonstrated something worth the consideration of men of wealth.

If Henry Ford is the master of the art of self-advertising — and he is that — much of it has been done in a manner to his credit. Some is not above criticism. He has discovered that he can compel the world to give him publicity the value of which cannot be estimated. But in that there is a danger which I think he fails to appreciate, — not to the world, but to him. It is a franchise which, if he fails to use wisely and with self-restraint, may prove his undoing, as it has proved the undoing of others.

The man who proceeds on the theory that it is a good thing to keep people talking about him, no matter what they say, will sooner or later waken up to the fact that the public is no longer interested even in the good and worth-while things he is doing and saying. Publicity of the kind Mr. Ford enjoys is a public franchise, and public franchises are sometimes withdrawn when not properly used.

# CHAPTER III

I HAVE said that we are interested in Henry Ford because of his phenomenal success in the field of industry.

But there is another reason, and that is that he has in him all the makings of a popular hero. A boy on a farm with a humble parentage back of him; never saw the inside of a college, and never was particularly interested in what went on inside a country schoolhouse; interested as a boy in steam engines and threshing machines; also in what is inside a watch and a clock; always dreaming of a self-propelled vehicle and drawing pictures of the same; builds a " farm locomotive " before he is twenty by mounting a steam engine on the cast-off wheels of a mowing machine; becomes the engineer of a steam threshing machine when a boy of seventeen; leaves the farm and gets a job in a power house in the city; works after hours on a gasoline engine, making the cylinder out of gas pipe, and the flywheel out of wood; puts the engine on a vehicle of his own construction that looks like a baby carriage; adds a few pulleys, a lever or two, and a leather belt, and the " darned thing ran." That first " gasoline buggy " is still in existence, and the " darned thing " still runs. It is kept in a room adjoining his office at Dearborn.

I have heard from him and Mrs. Ford the story of the last forty-eight hours that he worked on that first car. Forty-eight hours without sleep. The second night Mrs. Ford sat up waiting the outcome of his efforts. The machine was nearing completion. Would it run? It was about 2 a. m. when he came in from the little shop that stood in the rear of the house. The car was finished and ready for a try-out. It was raining. Mrs. Ford threw a cloak over her shoulders and followed him to the shop. He rolled the little car out into the alley, started it, mounted the seat and drove off. The car went a short distance and stopped. The trouble was a minor one. The nut of a bolt had come off. It seems that there was some vibration in that first machine which has been handed down to its millions of offspring. The car was put back in the shop. It had run. One of the foothills at the base of the mountain of success had been topped.

But there were other hills to climb, with valleys of discouragement between. People laughed at the strange device and at the man who created it. The noise it made resembled that of a machine gun in action. Instinctively, so it seemed, horses recognized in it the arch enemy of their race, took fright and ran away. Rumor has it that the police ordered him to keep the thing off the streets. Mr. Ford says this rumor is without foundation. Perhaps the wish of the people was father to the thought.

Whenever he drove this odd looking contrivance a curious crowd followed on bicycles, making uncomplimentary remarks. It was a " crazy thing," the outcome of a " crazy idea," born of a " half-cracked brain." It never would amount to anything. As a plaything, yes, it might be made to go on a hard, level road. But it never would prove of practical value as a means of travel.

On the East Grand Boulevard, in Detroit, there is a bridge over the Grand Trunk railroad tracks. The approach is up a fairly stiff grade. It was here the crowd was wont to assemble to see if Henry could made the grade. He made it. And he has been climbing ever since.

That little car, with its gas-pipe cylinders, wooden flywheel, and leather belt transmission, had all the mechanical principles in its make-up that enter into the present Ford car. It was on this car that he rested and won his famous Selden patent suit.

That first car was a crude affair. It certainly did not look like a million dollars. Those who looked at it thought a pile of money could be sunk in it, but they could not see how any ever could be gotten out of it. Money to develop and perfect his idea came in small sums, and for the most part from men of small means. Those who financed his genius and had the courage to stick came out with millions. Mr. Ford does not believe in stock companies now. They aren't necessary after you have made the grade.

One meets around Detroit now and then a man who, with hands in empty pockets, tells you with a sad, far-away look in his eyes, how he had a chance to put some money into the Ford company at the time it was being organized, " and just came within an ace of doin' it, too." Alas! the ace, whatever that means.

Henry Ford was, and still is, a dreamer. But as far back as the days of Joseph — and the greatest dreamers of the world, by the way, have been of Hebrew extraction — dreamers have not been held in high esteem by some of their brethren, especially in the days before their dreams came true. As a rule they climb alone a steep and stony path across which men delight in raising barriers. Dreamers upset the rules of prophecy. According to the laws of logic and the rules of men who walk by sight, these men who dream and move as in a sleep, should come to grief — and do not. I suppose the reason is that men who dream walk by faith, not by sight, and faith laughs at mountains. He who sees thinks he must remove the mountains that bar his way. He who dreams does not attempt to remove the mountains. He climbs them. And that after all is perhaps the best way to dispose of mountains.

Joseph lived to see his dream come true and to receive the homage of the men who ridiculed and hated him. Will Henry Ford pardon me for discovering this striking resemblance between himself and a man of a race in which he seems able to see so few virtues and so many faults?

# CHAPTER IV

## THE FORD FORTUNE

I do not know how much Henry Ford is worth. I am under the impression that, if he so desired, he could convert his business into a stock company and pay very satisfactory dividends on a billion capitalization. I doubt whether any other man ever made so large a fortune in so short a time. I believe it to be one of the cleanest, if not the cleanest, fortune of its size ever made.

As a rule, great wealth is quickly made by a gamble of some sort, or by investments in a highly favored and protected field, or by acquiring a monopoly of some natural resource, or by business methods which crush competition.

Henry Ford has made his money in a free, open, unprotected and competitive field.

The one possible blot on his record in this connection is the charge that he has sometimes dealt ruthlessly with smaller independent concerns which were making some parts of his car for him; that while he was paying his own labor a minimum wage of five and six dollars a day, he was demanding of others that they sell him their product at a price that made it impossible for them to pay their labor a fair wage; that he has encouraged men to make large investments in order to furnish him with materials, and then has suddenly ceased to place orders with them and left them with an idle investment and a deserted factory on their hands.

Perhaps his answer to this charge, if there is any truth in it, would be that even so, they made good money while they were going, and that he left them better off than when he found them; and as for the low wages paid their men, that was not due to the price he set for their output but to poor management and production methods; for later he was able to make the thing they were making for him at a cost less than he was paying them, and at the same time to pay five and six dollars minimum wage for the labor that went into it.

# THE FORD FORTUNE

I have listened to many discussions on this point and am well aware that there is a sharp division of opinion in regard to it. The view one takes of it will depend almost entirely on what he considers fair in business, and on that men are a long way from agreement.

Henry Ford does not gamble. I once saw him win five cents on a bet. I took it away from him and put it into a charity fund so I know that tainted nickel is not mixed up with the other twenty billion nickels, more or less, now in his possession.

I once ran him a foot race on which we and our friends risked a small stake. Henry won. And I may say right here for the benefit of others more than fifty years of age and forty-two inches in circumference that you are not in Mr. Ford's class unless you have kept in excellent physical condition.

And I may add also, by way of finishing this story, that Mr. Ford took the money from those who won on this race and gave it to an old gate-keeper at a railroad crossing.

But this is aside. What I started to say was that the Ford fortune, as fortunes go, is clean.

And it has been handled in a way that has caused neither criticism nor hatred on the part of the working classes. If there are any who would like to see Mr. Ford lose out, they are not in the ranks of labor.

He has been generous toward his employees. On this point I think I can speak with some authority, as I was in a position to know for a period of several years. During the time I was with the company he gave to his employees, in addition to a generous wage, more than a hundred million dollars out of his profits, all of which he could have retained as his own, and which the average man would have put into his own pocket.

It is said that his profit-sharing plan was a crafty scheme for getting more work out of his men; that it actually returned more dollars to him than he gave out. It was unquestionably a shrewd and profitable stroke. To the credit of Mr. Ford be it said that he personally never maintained that his profit and bonus schemes were a means for distributing charity.

I have often discussed the Ford Profit Sharing Plan before groups of employers of labor. Seldom, if ever, have I done so that some man has not risen to ask, " Didn't the plan pay? And didn't Mr. Ford believe that it would pay? Would he have instituted it, if he had not believed it would bring more dollars to him? " And the answer was, " Certainly the plan pays. That is just the point I am trying to make. And I would further like to make it clear that the plan is not copyrighted. Any employer is at liberty to try it. Both for the sake of the employer and the employees, we would like to see others try it out."

Labor in this country is said to be about forty per cent. efficient. If a more liberal grant of the earnings of labor were made to labor, possibly it would draw out enough of the unused sixty per cent. to make the experiment profitable to both labor and capital. That it would do so is, in my opinion, a fact that Henry Ford has proved to the industrial world. A man works best when he is working for his own interest. If Henry Ford from self-interest appeals to the self-interest in others, he is at least working along and in accordance with laws of human nature and is doing a better, fairer and more rational thing than if, for purely selfish purposes, he exploited his workers.

Since becoming rich Henry Ford has acquired no expensive tastes, formed no costly habits. He makes no display. As compared with the manner in which he might live, he may be said to live very plainly and simply. He has often said to me, "Wealth does not change men. The possession of it does not spoil them, as is so often claimed. Wealth simply reveals what there is in a man. It lifts the lid and gives what is in him a chance to come out. If the bad comes to the surface, it is because it was there and was only waiting for a chance to express itself."

He enjoys the quiet and seclusion of his home and family. He first built a home on Edison Avenue. About the same time other men who had gone into the automobile game, and were making far less money out of it than he, were building houses that might have been taken for the spawn of Rhine castles, if ever they had spawned. I once said to him that, judging from appearance so far as homes were concerned, the Ford Company could not be making as much money as some others.

" Well," he replied, " you know if I were going to live in a hotel, I would want some one else to run it. I prefer a home." And then after a pause, and with a chuckle, he added, " I still like boiled potatoes with the skins on, and I do not want a man standing back of my chair at table laughing up his sleeve at me while I am taking the potatoes' jackets off."

He still likes what he always liked. His personal habits and pleasures remain very much as they were in the days of his obscurity. Wealth has simply lifted the lid, and that which is coming out, according to his own theory, was always there.

There is a new home out on the banks of the Rouge in Dearborn. My wife and I were with him and Mrs. Ford the day the foundations for the new home were roughly staked out. Social ambition would have dictated a different locality. Sentiment of the finer sort said, " Here in the midst of scenes where we were boy and girl and lovers together; here in sight of the cottage which was the first modest home where dreams of the future were dreamed, and air castles that have since come down to earth were built; here among old friends who have known us all our lives will the new home be erected." And there it stands, large but not pretentious; not a hotel run by a regiment of servants, but a house in which to live in quiet and comfort, a home with the home atmosphere about it.

Some years before the new house was erected Mr. Ford said to me, " I have found something to inscribe over the fireplace in the new home when I build it." He then repeated the following, " Chop your own wood and it will warm you twice." And the words are there over one of the great open fireplaces in the Dearborn house. They express, or rather suggest, one fundamental article of his creed. It is the wholesome, saving power of work.

In speaking more particularly of the " downs and outs," he has often said to me, " You preach one gospel, and I another. My gospel is work. If a man is down and out, the only thing that will save him is work, —

work that will give him something to live on and to live for."

His conception of his relation to wealth he has stated to me in this way, " The money I have gathered together is not mine to do with altogether as I please. I do not own it. It is mine to control simply as the steward of it. The men who have worked with me have helped to create it. After they have had their wages and a share of the profits, it is my duty to take what remains and put it back into industry in order to create more work for more men at higher pay."

Henry Ford's passion, so far as wealth is concerned, is not to own it, but to create it. I think him sincere in his statement when he says that his ambition is not to make millions, but to make opportunities for the employment of labor.

" If I were as rich as Henry Ford " — so have I heard a thousand penniless dreamers begin the unfolding of a powerful charitable or philanthropic scheme. And Henry's one answer to them all is, " My gospel is work. The best use to which I can put my money is to make more work for more men." And while Henry lives the Ford fortune is likely to be handled with that as the main object in view.

# CHAPTER V

## SOME ELEMENTS OF SUCCESS

HENRY FORD has built up a great industry;
he has amassed a great fortune; he has paid
labor a liberal wage; he has built a hospital;
he has set in operation agencies which in their
day have done a great deal of good. To human thought, to politics, to science, the arts,
education, religion, his contribution — directly
or indirectly — is yet to be made.

What he has done for others has been along
lines that have as a rule brought a liberal return to himself. Seriously and to his credit I
would say that his most valuable contribution
to humanity thus far has been his discovery
of some very profitable kinds of philanthropy.
A good thing done for reward is good. Nobler
and better things, however, are possible. I
wish Henry Ford had more good to his credit
that had cost him something. In actual service to humanity and in unselfish use of his

wealth his old running mate, Couzens, has done so far more that will live.

Henry Ford plays a spectacular game. He pulls some wonderful stunts. He is a pinch hitter in finance and the idol of the bleachers. But there are better all-round men in the game. He is as temperamental as an artist and as erratic. He has been known to fan out. And he certainly muffed a couple of balls in the case of the Peace Ship and his Jewish diatribes. He is not a team man. He must play the game alone and for himself. He has advanced a good many men on the bases of the financial diamond, but I do not recall that he ever did so by a sacrifice hit.

Henry Ford has attained a remarkable prominence, but he has not attained that which makes prominence permanent, namely, eminence. Prominence may be gained by saying things and doing things; eminence is achieved by being. The essence of eminence is in a man — in his mind and soul. Henry Ford is an unusual, a most remarkable man, but not a great man — not yet. There are in him neither that breadth nor depth of mind, nor that moral grandeur which are the distinguishing marks of the truly great. Some men are born great, some achieve greatness, but no man ever had greatness thrust upon him, Shakespeare to the contrary. He may be thrust into prominence, but not into eminence, for eminence is reached by climbing an inward spiritual ascent.

If Henry Ford could quit watching the popular winds, take down his political lightning rod, and devote himself to the solution of those human problems which press upon him for solution as an industrial leader, I think he could attain a great and enviable reputation. It is in that direction, I believe, that he will find the fulfillment of the wish which he expressed to me when he said, " I do not want the things which can be bought with money. I want to live a life — to live so that the world will be better for my having lived in it." He has had the vision. He has the ability and the opportunity.

It is unfortunate that he has not manifested the same sustained interest in the work undertaken in behalf of his employees that he has shown in some other matters. In some things he reveals an indomitable will, an unfailing interest. In other things the will weakens and the interest dies. He sometimes springs at things with startling suddenness. And then he drops them as suddenly as he took them up. It requires a stronger will to be than to do.

In 1914 he entered with great enthusiasm a new path in the field of social justice. The work he then instituted gave promise of a notable contribution to human progress along industrial lines. It quickened the conscience of the employers. It roused hope in the ranks of labor. It promised the restoration of that which modern industry has lost and which would prove the greatest boon any man could restore to it, namely, a personal relation between employer and employee. That phase of the work, with some other distinguishing features of it, are for the present in eclipse; only in eclipse, it is to be hoped.

As to Henry Ford's success in industry, it is no mere accident. You cannot say that it is a matter of luck that a man's boat is floated by the rising tide, if he has carefully calculated the time the tide comes in and has built his boat where it would be caught and carried out to sea.

Mr. Ford anticipated the rising tide of the automobile industry. He must be given credit for that. Credit also is due him for the way in which he deliberately planned to take the fullest possible advantage of the tide when it came in. Standardization is his hobby. He would have all shoes made on one last, all hats made on one block, and all coats according to one pattern. It would not add to the beauty of life, but it would greatly reduce the cost of living.

When it came to automobiles Henry Ford decided to make them all alike and of a size that would fit, not the greatest number of people, but the largest number of pocketbooks. Keep your eye on the average pocketbook. That was his slogan. Only a few people can buy what they want. The vast majority buy what they can afford. No one was ever able to shake him in his decision to make one car, the best of its kind that can be made for the money, suited to the bank roll of the greatest number of people, standardized so as to admit of quantity production and therefore of manufacture at minimum cost.

Once he got going he discovered and put into practice some very profitable ways of being generous. His division of profits with his employees paid in dollars and cents. That fact made it none the less a boon to labor. His policy of sharing some of his profits with the consumer by cutting the price of the car also paid. It widened his market and won the confidence and good-will of the public. He did what no other man has ever been able to do, — touched the hearts of the people through their pocketbooks.

He never went to college, but he knows all the psychology there is to know in so far as it has to do with the dollar.

Most conspicuous among the things which have entered into his success are those of courage and tenacity. His courage has not always been guided by the best of judgment, but on the whole it has won him more than it has lost. His tenacity borders at times on obstinacy and is coupled with a cool patience that seems to render him indifferent to the passing of time.

He seems to shrink from encounters in which it will be necessary for him to say unpleasant things. In other words, he hates a quarrel but he loves a good fight. He is of Irish descent. He keeps his eye on his opponent — many eyes on him, in fact — and is master in the art of waiting. This is one of the reasons why I think he enjoys lawsuits, of which he has had his share: they are usually so long drawn out. There are so many courts of appeal, and the more the merrier.

At times he wearied of the Selden patent trial, but when the bell rang for a new round he always came back smiling and full of fight. The Dodge trial dragged a weary length; the *Tribune* trial was long drawn out; the Newberry fight extended over a period of several years. These are illustrations of his bulldog grip, once he takes hold. He may consume so much time in the accomplishment of a thing that you think he has forgotten all about it, and he may travel in so many devious ways to reach his end that you think he has turned aside

47

to other things, but he never forgets. The long years of struggle against poverty and ridicule in the development of his car is the evidence of the presence in him of a quality to be admired by his friends, but to be most seriously and fearfully contemplated by his enemies.

# CHAPTER VI

A cross section of the mind of Henry Ford would reveal some striking contrasts. There are in him mental altitudes which mark him as a genius, and there are others that are little above mental sea level. A complex mind of strength and weakness, of wisdom and foolishness, in which the shallows are the more pronounced because of the profound depths which lie between.

Mr. Ford has limitations which stand out the more conspicuously because of the far reaches of his mind in other directions. He has altogether a most unusual mind, — in some respects the most remarkable mind I have ever known. Call it insight, intuition, vision or what you please, he has a supernormal perceptive faculty along certain lines in business affairs.

His mind does not move in logical grooves. It does not walk, it leaps.

It is not a trained mind. It does not know how to think consecutively, and I doubt if it would do so if it could. It cannot endure the pace and bear the burden of logic, and it cannot listen long to the man who is reaching conclusions through rational processes. I have known him frequently to cut in and give a man a decision before he has had time to state his case, and sometimes the decision has had nothing whatever to do with the case. Under such circumstances there was no use trying to get the real problem before him. A later opportunity must be waited for.

He does not reason to conclusions. He jumps at them. A bad thing, unless the jump, as in his case, is as a rule more unerring than the slow reasoned crawl of other minds. He has told me that he learned early in life " to grab the first hunch." His first impulses, so he insists, are as a rule to be relied upon and acted upon. He maintains that if he stops to reason about them, to discuss them, to seek advice regarding them, he finds them trimmed, pared and filed down until they fit into the conventional ruts, and there is nothing left that is really worth doing.

Concerning matters in general he seems to enjoy a discussion, but concerning matters pertaining to his own business on which his mind is made up — and it generally is — he seems annoyed by opposing opinion. " Get out, and send me an optimist," he once said to an executive who was venturing to question the wisdom of some policy decided upon. " I want to talk to an optimist." And that gives you another definition of an optimist; he is the man who agrees with you.

He has the courage of his convictions, and I have never known him to change his mind on an important matter, once it was made up. Minds that work intuitively, I have observed, have a feeling of finality in regard to their decisions, — the feminine mind on occasions, for example. It is so because — it is so. And there is an end to the matter. This, in my opinion, is the chief reason for the high rate of mortality among Ford executives. As you know, the rate is high.

# HENRY FORD

The Ford executive has added to those two certainties in life — taxes and death — a third, that is discharge. Of the man climbing up in the Ford organization it may be said that he hath but a short time to live and is full of misery. He cometh up and is cut down like a flower. He never continueth for long on the job.

A judge of national repute once said to me, " I have a great admiration for Henry Ford, but there is one thing about him that I regret and can't understand, and that is his inability to keep his executives and old-time friends about him." The answer is that it is not a matter of inability, but disability. He can't help it. He is built that way.

It is my impression that in business organizations men are hired as executives and paid among other things for their judgment and advice. The greatest possible liberty of thought and action is given an executive in the Ford Motor Company that can be given in a company that is a one-man affair and is controlled by a one-way mind. Mr. Ford's favorite executive seems to be the man who does not think, either from choice or lack of ability, and does what he is told to do regardless of consequences. In addition to this, so I have been told by those who enjoy his special favor, one must maintain an attitude toward the employees that makes them fear and hate you. " I am the most fortunate man in this organization, because every one despises me," is the way one of them put it to me. The theory seems to be that because the employees dislike you, you must be a whale of an executive. It is not every man that is so constituted that he cares to pay the price asked for a position of this kind. There are those who get more pleasure in running a business of their own in a way that wins respect and enables them to enjoy a few friendships.

A college trained man is not handicapped in the Ford Motor Company on that account, provided he does not place too much emphasis on the fact. Mr. Ford has his own theory of education. I have never heard him express any regret over his own limited opportunities.

It is possible that an untrained man, in attempting that which a trained and cautious man would not, may stumble upon things, make discoveries, the trained man would not be likely to make. The fools who rush in where angels fear to tread are at least in possession of some experience, if not some facts, entirely unknown to the angels.

A man may be a very ignorant man from the college student's point of view and still be a very wise man. It is not that a man is ignorant of the things that are taught in the schools that counts against him, but rather being ignorant of these things he sometimes suffers on account of his lack of knowledge of his own limitations. If Henry Ford knew his limitations he undoubtedly would not have attempted some things which have impaired his reputation. However, I am inclined to think that it is just as well that all men do not go to college. Now and then an original mind escapes the suppression of its originality by conventional training. I am sure that many parsons would have better mental light and ventilation if they had not had the windows of their minds filled up with stained glass in theological seminaries. I have met men who,

# TRAITS AND CHARACTERISTICS

I am sure, are more interesting for having grown up without scholarly inhibitions. In the case of Henry Ford, however, I am inclined to believe that the gains would have more than offset the losses.

There is one peculiar danger to which men of wealth untrained in the scholastic sense are exposed: the danger of assuming that because they have made a great success and shown exceptional ability in one field of action, therefore their opinions are of equal weight in all others. It does not follow, because a man has worked up from a job as section hand to that of railroad president, that he is a final authority on beetles and butterflies. It does not follow, because a man without training has made important scientific and mechanical discoveries, that he has the last word to say on religion and philosophy. Mr. Ford now and then enters fields of action for which he has not the special fitness that distinguishes him in his own particular field. But it is human to desire a wider scope for the exercise of our faculties. Even parsons in some instances feel peculiarly fitted to give big business men a lot of advice.

Mr. Ford is not the illiterate man that some have maliciously tried to make him out. His reading is limited, but he reads, — not the heavy tomes of history, philosophy, political science, and the like, but what for the want of a better name I would call the life books. He once gave me a volume in which he had inscribed his name. He gave it to me, he said, because he considered it one of the greatest books he had ever read. It was Drummond's "Greatest Thing in the World."

One Sunday afternoon I found him curled up on the sofa reading Emerson.

"How do you like him?" he was asked.

"Oh," he replied with a chuckle, "Emerson is a pup."

"Why a pup?"

"Well," he said, "I just get comfortably settled down to the reading of him when he uses a word I do not understand, and that makes me get up and look for a dictionary."

The law of compensation — whether he got the idea from Emerson or not, I do not know — is a favorite theme with him. Faith and optimism are also favorite subjects. He frequently repeats St. Paul's definition of faith. And faith and optimism in business have certainly figured in his success.

I would not leave the impression that Henry Ford is a diligent reader of Holy Scripture, or a student of Emerson. He is neither. As a manufacturer he is naturally immersed in a sea of practical affairs to the surface of which there rise once in a while bubbles of mysticism, haunting suggestions of " The Plan," a shadowy, Calvinistic belief in Fate or Foreordination, the serenities of one conscious of being a Child of Destiny. But his vast material interests are first. He is more interested in things than in thoughts. He perhaps reads a blue-print more readily and more understandingly than he reads Tolstoy, Darwin, Maeterlinck and Emerson. There are hundreds of men figuring prominently in the business world of no greater erudition than he, but on matters with which they are not familiar they have the gift of silence and a correspondingly low visibility.

# CHAPTER VII

## "JUST KIDS"

HENRY FORD was born July 30, 1863, and is still a boy. Along with the amazing shrewdness in him there is a charming simplicity. "How did he impress you?" I asked a well-known writer after she had an interview with Mr. Ford. "He is a mixture," she replied, "of sweetness and steel, of vision and practical shrewdness, of humor and authority, and of belief — belief in men, in nature." The steel is there — I have witnessed it strike and cut with the sparks flying from it — and also the sweetness. Children especially call forth the sweetness, the gentleness, the spirit of youth, the love of nature which are present in him. As between youth and age, he seems to prefer the company of youth. Introduce him to a group of people in which there are ninety-nine adults and one child, and the one child will receive the major portion of his attention and besides that will have a bully good time.

I have known him to spend the better part of a day in the woods with a boy of ten, and both were apparently having the time of their lives. "Come with me, boy," he said; "I want to show you some of my friends."

We were in a little cottage in the edge of the woods on the banks of the Rouge just above Mr. Ford's residence at Dearborn. He slipped a pair of opera glasses into his pocket and he and the boy started out on a "hike." I was not included in the invitation but decided to join what I knew would be an interesting expedition of exploration. A few rapid strides and then a pause.

"Listen, boy. Hear it? Hear it? Hear that song? Quiet, now! Don't move. He's right there in that tree somewhere." And out came the opera glasses. "Ah, there he is! I found him. Take the glasses, boy, and look at him. He's on the very tip of that limb. He's a beauty, isn't he?" There were feathered friends everywhere. He protects them the year round, feeds them in winter, knows their song, and calls them by name.

He loves the birds. How much, I once discovered on going to his home for dinner. The front door was locked. From the inside he called to us, informing us that it would be necessary to go to a rear entrance to gain admittance. Later the manner of our reception was explained. A robin had built her nest on the veranda over the front door. Entrance through that portal disturbed Mrs. Robin so much that Henry had nailed up the screen and locked the door until the Robin family had moved to other quarters.

But to return to my story.

As we passed through the fields I noticed what I thought were the foundations of numerous haystacks. Rails had been laid down on the ground several feet apart. Across these and close together other rails had been placed. On these, grass had been piled up to the depth of two or three feet.

" You must have had a wonderful crop of hay on this field," I remarked, " judging from the number of foundations for the stacks."

A merry twinkle came into his eye and he laughed as he said:

"Those are not foundations for haystacks. I had those built as shelters for the rabbits. It makes a nice warm place for them in which to live in the winter."

But his friends the rabbits abused his hospitality and came to a sad end. For once in his life, Henry Ford had to declare war and take up arms. It was a war to extermination. The increase of the rabbit population on the Ford farms taxed the agility and capacity of the multiplication table to its limit. To the saying "Pigs is pigs" may be added the further statement, "So is rabbits." After two or three years, orchards young and old were being destroyed by Friend Rabbit to such an extent that friendly relations were broken off and hostilities begun. Down to the last rabbit, bunny remained a pacifist; but somehow that did not stop the war. And perhaps this might be made into a parable.

After passing the rabbit shelters we came, a little farther on, to a cornfield in which the bare stalks of last year's crop were still standing.

" Why did you not cut this field of corn?" I asked.

Again there was a little chuckle, as he answered, " Well, you see, I planted that corn for the squirrels, and some of my other friends, and left it standing so they could get at it in the winter. And let me show you what they did."

We followed him a little way into the woods and found the ground covered with cobs from which the corn had been stripped.

" I have a lot of friends in here," he said. " Let me show you a particular friend. See that bird box — the one on the pole? Notice that the box is fastened to a straight, smooth rod of iron, and the iron is bolted to the top of the pole. I did that so the squirrels could not get at the birds. But see what happened. A flying squirrel took possession of that box and made it his home. He runs out on that limb that hangs over the box and makes a flying leap. He never fails to land on the roof of his home. I'll bet he's in there now. He knows my signal, and if he is there he'll come out and take a look. Now, boy, keep your eye on the hole in the box."

He went to the pole to the top of which the box was fastened. He rapped upon it — three times — and then out came the head of Friend Squirrel. For a minute he eyed us very calmly and very solemnly and then turned back to his nest as if satisfied that everything was all right, and that Henry and another boy were just making a friendly call.

And so the multimillionaire spent the better part of the day with a ten-year-old boy having a bully time calling on his furred and feathered friends. He loves the great outdoors. Beneath the fire and steel in him there is a boyish, joyous spirit. It is one of the lights that falls among the shadows.

I have referred elsewhere to the fact that Mr. Ford makes his most intimate counselors men in his own organization with whom it would seem he would have the least in common. That there is in Mr. Ford that which is attractive to men of a higher order is seen in the intimate friendship he has enjoyed with two great men—John Burroughs, up until the time of his death, and Thomas A. Edison. These three were in the habit of taking their annual outing together and were not infrequently together between times. What is there in common among them?

Between Burroughs and Ford there was the love of nature, of birds and flowers and streams and hills. One loved far more understandingly than the other, but both loved the same things.

Between Edison and Ford there is the bond of mechanics and invention. And back of it all there is the spirit of youth. It was in Burroughs to his last hour. It is in Edison and Ford. Edison at seventy-five is working his two shifts and finding his joy in life and his interest in his work increasing rather than diminishing.

"When are you going to retire?" he was asked recently. The reply was, "Never."

There is a story of Ford and Edison that has never gotten into print. It has an amusing and at the same time a dramatic incident in it that makes it worth repeating.

Late in the fall of 1914 Mr. Ford planned to take Mr. Edison by special train over the route between Detroit and Port Huron on which Edison in his youth had worked as newsboy. The train consisted of three or four coaches, and the party was limited to a small number of invited guests of whom I chanced to be one.

The trip to Port Huron was uneventful. Mr. Ford and Mr. Edison spent much of the time swapping stories; Mr. Edison recalling incidents of his boyhood days, and Mr. Ford offering a story now and then in which the laugh was on himself. One of Mr. Ford's stories on himself is also worth mention.

He, together with some of his mechanics, was testing a car some years ago, and to give it a thorough trial they made a trip over the sandy roads of Northern Michigan. They took an outfit with them and camped at night along the way. One evening they turned into a small wood a short distance from a farmhouse. On going to the house for some provisions they found the farmer in the barn tinkering with a second-hand automobile, not a Ford, by the way, but a much larger car. Without making himself known Mr. Ford inquired as to the nature of the trouble with the farmer's machine. The explanation was that the farmer had bought the car from an agent who had driven it to the farmer's home, and that he had never been able to get the thing started. Mr. Ford, with his mechanics, set to work, put the machine into running order, and contributed a few new spark plugs and some tools. When they had finished the farmer turned to Mr. Ford and said:

" What's the charge? "

" Nothing," was the reply.

" But I can't let it stand that way," said the farmer. " You have not only given your time, but you have also given me spark plugs and tools. Here's a dollar and a half. I insist you take that much at any rate."

" No," said Mr. Ford. " I can't do it. I have all the money I want."

The old farmer looked him over and then drawled out, " Hell, you can't have much and drive a Ford car."

Mr. Ford left without disclosing his identity.

Arriving in Port Huron, Mr. Ford decided to give to Mr. Edison a new start in his old business. He purchased from a newsboy his entire outfit, — basket, papers, apples, oranges, chewing gum, crackerjack and all the rest, and had it smuggled aboard our train.

As we were pulling out a son of Mr. Edison brought the basket to his father and holding it up before him, said, " Here you are, Dad. Go to it."

Edison hooked his arm through the handle of the basket and began to call his wares. Down through the train he went, doing a land-office business, for everybody bought, and Edison gave back no change. I have before me as I write a copy of the *El Paso Herald,* which I purchased from the newsboy Edison. It cost me a dollar. It is worth more than that to-day.

The boys — Henry and Thomas — were having a great time. Henry was missing for a while and when he returned it was with face and hands black from smoke and coal dust. " The engineer on this train," he explained, " is an old friend of mine. I knew him when I worked at the electric light plant. So I have been having a visit with him. I went forward, climbed over the tender and down into the cab. I've been running the engine."

It was dark when we reached Mt. Clemens. It was in the little station house here that Edison had worked as a telegraph operator. A stop was made that he might take a look at the place in which dreams were dreamed which in after years became realities. While in the station Henry suggested that Thomas send a message over the wire. The agent cleared the wire and Edison seated himself at the instrument. Slowly he began to tick off a message to a son at home in New Jersey. It was one of those moments that leaves on one an indelible impression. A group of people stood in silence looking at a man then close to seventy years of age, but in imagination seeing the boy of many years ago.

Suddenly some operator down the road broke in on the wire. Edison paused and listened. A smile played about his mouth. The operator who was standing behind Mr. Edison and had been leaning over him, silently watching his slow and deliberate work at the key, turned suddenly and gave those of us standing about a look which passed rapidly through the emotions of embarrassment, shame, anger and horror. Then he smiled and said to us, "Some operator has broken in and sent over the wire the message, ' Tell that kid to get off the line.' "

And he was right. There was a " kid " on the line. And there was another one back of him, enjoying the fun.

When Mr. Edison had finished, the operator sat down at the key and sent the information down the line that the " kid " who had just slowly ticked off the lazy message was Thomas A. Edison, " apprentice operator on this key more than fifty years ago."

I would give a great deal to know just what that fellow who broke in on Edison's message thinks of himself as a practical joker.

# CHAPTER VIII

### BEHIND A CHINESE WALL

ONCE you get to Mr. Ford, you will find him, of all men, most affable and democratic. He is apt to leave upon you the impression that he stands ready to do anything for you, give you anything, even to the half of his kingdom. He makes promises which he sometimes keeps, sometimes forgets, and sometimes fulfills in his own peculiar way. He hates to say " No." He has a way of leaving you with the idea that he is in entire sympathy with your proposition and of delegating the unpleasant task of turning you down to some one else.

To turn down a request made of us is embarrassing. To grant a favor is a pleasure. Henry Ford is a man of generous impulses. I think he would prefer on all occasions to do what he is asked to do. This, of course, is impossible. And so, when it is necessary to turn a man down, he seeks to relieve himself of the embarrassment of doing so by referring the man to some one else, at the same time indicating just how he would have the man and his request handled. He has sometimes given a man a note to an executive, which was in reality a code letter understood by the official receiving it. That note was always the same with slight variations in the spelling of one word. The fate of the individual joyfully and unsuspectingly bearing that note hung on the spelling of that word. If the note read " Please s-e-e this man," it meant he was to be favorably handled. If it read " Please s-e-a this man," it meant that he was to be let down as easy as possible, — dropped overboard into a sea of uncertainty, so far as obtaining what he wanted was concerned, there to wait and flounder about until, utterly discouraged, he gave up hope of attaining his end. It always seemed to me that a blunt " No " would have been a much more considerate way of dealing with cases of this kind.

Genial, generous and democratic will be found the manner of Henry Ford, once you get to him, but the problem is to get to him.

The approach to him is, I believe, the most guarded and most difficult of that of any man alive. He would have it so. People who do not understand blame his secretary for making this man of the people so inaccessible. But his secretary is to be praised for the thoroughness with which he does the work assigned him. A Chesterfield might suggest that which here and there would add grace and charm to the manner in which the job is handled but he certainly could do nothing to raise the present standard of efficiency.

Hardly a week passes that some one does not come to me from a distance with the request that I be kind enough to assist him in obtaining an interview with Mr. Ford. The answer is, " There is but one approach to Mr. Ford and that is through his secretary." And then the question, " How do I get to his secretary?" And the answer is, " Make an appointment with him and take your knitting along. You may have to wait."

Socially, Henry Ford has preferred to remain in the class in which he was born. He goes occasionally into the drawing-rooms of those who have attained social distinction, but he is not at ease there and remains no longer than is necessary.

Detroit has three aristocracies of the kind that bears upon its shield the rampant dollar sign. A landed aristocracy, descended from the early French settler whose farms fronted on the river and extended in a narrow strip inland two or three miles; the aristocracy based on the wealth drawn from Michigan's forests and minerals; and in these latter days, an automobile aristocracy, — the product of the automobile industry. Henry Ford has stormed the doors of none of them.

People in all walks of life and of all ranks come from near and far to see him. But the vast majority fail to attain the object of their visit, due to the Chinese Wall about him, erected and guarded by his secretary. Those who do see him have, as a rule, paid for the privilege in hours and sometimes in days of waiting. If all the hours men have spent in waiting to see Henry Ford were added together it would be interesting to know just how many thousands of years the grand total would represent. No king was ever so hedged about, none but the Grand Llama of Thibet was ever so inaccessible.

Henry Ford would be a greater and wiser man if he were a better mixer and listener. An insulated mind in an isolated body misses much in this world that is really worth knowing.

But I cannot say that I altogether blame him for his aloofness from the world. Every man with a crank's turn of mind; promoters of every description; social and political dreamers of all kinds; inventors of hairpins, market baskets and perpetual motion; of accessories for the Ford car, enough of them to require a trailer to carry them; big men seeking millions and little men wanting enough money to pay the rent; representatives of the church, the college and the university; builders of homes for stray cats and hospitals for dogs; writers seeking an annuity so that they may give their time without anxiety to literary pursuits; experts in sociology who would like to be put on an allowance so as to be able to give him the benefit of their wisdom in the solution of his industrial problems and work out ways for the philanthropic expenditure of his millions; experts who propose to solve all problems by making the paper-pulp supply of the world take the place of gold as a monetary basis, — these and others too numerous to mention have made a beaten path to his door, not because Emerson's magical mousetrap is there, but because the philosopher's stone, that turns so much vanadium steel into gold, is there and is to them an irresistible lodestone. They have heard of Henry Ford as the friend of man, and they feel sure he will finance anything they have to offer.

Wherever he goes the crowds press upon him as if he were a king out for an airing and thrust their petitions, not into his hands, but into his ears. I once took him to a reception at which a large number of high dignitaries of the church were present. They formed in line, like purchasers of tickets at a circus, and in turn made their wants known for schools, colleges, missions and struggling parishes. He left that reception with a pocket full of cards on which were noted the amounts of money and the number of Ford cars each ecclesiastic could use in his business. I have seen him besieged in a similar manner by business men at club receptions. I can understand Henry Ford's aversion to polite society. I do not altogether blame him for preferring to live behind a Chinese Wall.

And let no one think he has gotten to him when, by hook or crook, he has gotten over or under or through the wall. Back of the wall and beyond the moat stands the castle of his mind. It is a mind that prefers to think its own thoughts and to choose its own themes for conversation. You want to see Henry Ford? He will see you, — not to talk about the thing you wish to talk about, but to tell you something he has to say to you. You fence and jockey in a vain attempt to turn the conversation in the direction of the matter for which you have sought the interview.

I recall, by way of illustration, an interview which two men had with him at his own home. It was by appointment and was in regard to a contribution to a church building fund. "What success did you have?" I asked one of them the next day. " We had a delightful visit," he replied. " Mr. Ford entertained us and so led the conversation that we never got a chance to mention the church."

During the war three men came all the way from New York to see him on camp recreational work. They had insisted on an interview, and he had finally told them that if they came to Detroit he would see them. They came. He met them. Then he came to me and said, " You take these fellows and talk to them. I told them that if they came I would see them. I have seen them. I met them and said ' good morning ' when they came in. That is all they will see of me. When you are through with them, turn them over to my secretary." He kept his word. They had " seen " Henry Ford and returned to New York without putting their cause before him.

He speaks at times with the air of great finality, as a man who has received a revelation or has secret sources of information on the great subjects of the day. He talks in short, broken, disconnected sentences. And he has a way of discoursing on one of his favorite themes — Wall Street, the Jew, international bankers sitting in secret conclave somewhere and planning another war, world peace through farm tractors and water power, the synthetic cow — in a way that produces among his listeners a profound and embarrassing silence, broken occasionally by a remark from one of his two or three familiars, whose words of approval do not always leave the impression that they are speaking out of the depths of knowledge or profound conviction.

Men of great wealth and limited education often fail to appreciate the fact that they are in danger of overestimating the worth of their judgment on matters outside the industrial world in which they live. Few men have the courage to argue with a millionaire, — especially if they chance to be in the dependent position of employees. This silence, or at least veiled expression of opinion on the part of those thrown in daily contact with a man of wealth, is likely to leave upon him the impression that he is an oracle on anything he chooses to talk about.

The isolation of Henry Ford's mind is about

as near perfect as it is possible to make it. For this reason the confidence born in him of success along one line never forsakes him when he enters other spheres of thought and action. Adverse criticism reaches him, of course, but it does not penetrate. And when one is working on the theory that it is better to be the subject of adverse criticism than none at all what hope is there that any dart ever will reach him?

# CHAPTER IX

## HENRY FORD AND THE CHURCH

I ONCE preached a sermon for Henry Ford's special benefit. I told him I was going to do so and asked him to be present and hear it. He came. He listened very attentively. He went away. It was a good sermon, if I do say it myself, but so far as I was ever able to see it never fazed him. It came about in this way:

Mr. and Mrs. Ford were members of my parish. I was building a new church, a Gothic structure, that was costing considerable money. The building had been under way for some time and Mr. Ford had made no contribution toward the cost of its construction. This somewhat nettled certain of my parish. "What is the matter with your friend, Mr. Ford, that he does not help us out on this matter? Every one is giving up to the limit, and he, the richest man in the parish, has done nothing." This question and statement of fact were put up to me a good many times.

Finally two members of my vestry, against my advice, decided to call on Mr. Ford and solicit a subscription to the building fund. They went, spent a pleasant evening with him, talked for the most part about almost everything but the one thing they went to him to talk about, because he steered the conversation, and came away, as I have stated in another chapter, empty handed.

One of the gentlemen who interviewed Mr. Ford on this occasion was himself a man of wealth and very generous toward his church. After telling me of what took place at the interview, he launched into a severe criticism of Ford. I stopped him. " You say that Henry Ford is wanting in generosity," I said to him. " Well, do you know that there are people in this city who say the same thing of you?"

" How can they say that?" he said, evidently somewhat nettled. " You know that it is not true. You know that I have given thousands, tens of thousands, to my church and its institutions."

" I know that," I replied, " and that is just the point people make against you. They say your church is your hobby. You give to it, but in the opinion of the public you give relatively little or nothing to anything else."

" But it's my money, isn't it? Am I not at liberty to give it away as I deem best? If I want to give it all to the church, whose business is it but my own?" was his reply.

" Why then criticize Henry Ford," I replied, " for claiming exactly the same privilege when he comes to giving his money away? He is giving millions to his employees. You give to your church. He does not believe in your way of doing things, and you do not believe in his methods. Personally, I think the world needs both of you, that both are doing a service to humanity, and I am not going to allow either of you to criticize the other in my presence without a protest."

A short time afterward Mr. Ford referred to the visit which he had from the two members of my vestry. " I don't believe in building big and costly churches for the rich," he said, in explaining his refusal to contribute toward the erection of the building then under way. " The amount of money you are putting into this one church edifice would provide for a half dozen settlement houses which, if properly placed, would do a great deal more good."

It was then that I told him that if he would come to church the next Sunday and give me a chance to talk to him when he could not talk back, I would tell him why I thought the centers of worship should be as beautiful and costly as men could make them. He said he would come. And he did.

" There is a man in this city," so the sermon ran, in part, " who has done a very unusual thing. You know that power houses are built, as a rule, in the rear of factories. Often they are just dark, dusty, greasy holes in the ground, with mountains of coal piled outside. Factory buildings and office buildings are put out on the street and much thought is given to their appearance. The power plant is put in a squat building, often in a shed, on the rear of the lot. But the man to whom I refer has done differently. He has built the costliest and most beautiful power house in America. He has put it on the avenue along with the office building. He has filled the windows with plate glass. He has tiled the floors. Outside and in, that building is rubbed, scrubbed, washed and polished.

"I can imagine people criticizing this man for the thing he has done. Why spend so much money on a building which is to shelter nothing but the boilers and engines of a plant? Something far less costly would have answered the purpose. Instead of engines with flywheels, which do nothing but go round and round, why did he not put some of his wonderful automatic machines, which do something, out in front, where people could see them, and relegate the power plant to the rear?

" The answer is, men spend money on the things they love and value. The buildings we erect are symbols of our pride in and affection for the things inside. What a man thinks of his home is revealed in the kind of house he builds around it. What a man thinks of his business is shown in the buildings he erects to house it. This man I have in mind was born with a love for mechanical things. The power that makes them go is a thing which, to him, is worthy of a shelter as costly and as beautiful as he can afford to make it. The energy that throbs through the great factory he knows comes from the power house, where the ponderous flywheels turn in comparative silence. The power house is back of it all; that is why he made it the costly, beautiful thing it is.

" And that is why I am going to put all the money I can get into this church. It is the spiritual power house back of all the fine things men are doing in the way of service. It stands for that which should be symbolized in costly and beautiful ways. And in that way men, who understand it and love it, will be glad to see it housed."

Some time later, on an Easter morning, a check was placed on the plate designated for the building fund. I never credited it to the sermon; the sermon was worth more.

But when it came to a building for the social activities of the parish, it was different. " That's a good thing," Mr. Ford said to me.

" I want to give to that." And he voluntarily gave liberally to it. He came back to the subject of this work at a later time and insisted on making a second contribution which was larger than I felt it wise to accept. It doesn't often happen, but I have known churches to be destroyed by the generosity of a few rich people. I wanted to avoid that.

Mrs. Ford does much through the regular channels of the church and charity organizations. To her personal interest and wise guidance the Ford Hospital owes more than the public ever will know. To her generosity the Williams House, a church institution and a temporary home for border-line girls, owes its establishment. There are many who could speak as recipients of her private and individual charity.

Through the mails countless appeals for help come to her. And conscientiously and with a woman's sympathy she goes laboriously through these letters herself. Numerous cases she has turned over to me for investigation through my department. The pity of it is that so many proved to be undeserving. Great was the surprise and confusion of people to find that their letters had touched the sympathy which they had hoped to arouse, but that that sympathy proposed to act intelligently. No case, if it seemed to merit investigation, was turned down by Mrs. Ford.

There is a woman on a farm in Arkansas, for example, who must be still wondering at the reach of the Ford Motor Company, because an investigator appeared at her door one day in answer to her pitiful appeal to Mrs. Ford. And she must still experience some embarrassment when she recalls how widely her real condition, as the investigator found it to be, differed from her description of it in her letter to Mrs. Ford. She was well to do, but Arkansas seemed such a long way from Dearborn that she thought she could take a chance on getting something without her case being looked into.

The personal attention which Mrs. Ford gives to these cases is but an index of the gentleness, the kindness, and sympathy that are in her as well as of the thorough and intelligent manner in which she does her work.

But to return to Mr. Ford and the church. Frequently are the questions asked, " Is he a churchman? " " Is he a Christian? " " What are his religious views? " "Is he a religious man? "

These seem to be the same question put in a little different form, but they are not. The information sought in each case is far from the same. Each question reveals, all unconsciously, a peculiar religious " slant " in the mind of the person asking it.

If to the one who asks the first question you state the fact that Mr. Ford was baptized and confirmed in the Episcopal Church, he is quite satisfied. He has gotten all the information concerning Mr. Ford's religion he wants. He belongs to a church. Then he is all right.

The man who asks the second question is not, so I have discovered, particularly interested in Mr. Ford's church affiliations. What he wants to know is something about the individual moral standards of Mr. Ford and the character of his private life. When you tell him that Mr. Ford's private life is clean, his tastes are simple, his pleasures are wholesome, and that he loves and enjoys his home, you have told him what he wants to know.

The man who asks the third question is just burning up to know if Mr. Ford is a Theosophist, a Spiritualist, or a New Thoughter. Does he believe in transmigration of the soul, or in reincarnation? What does he think of Confucius, and Buddha? Would it be possible to have a talk with him on the esoteric teachings of the ancient mystics, or the doctrine of the Stoics? Inasmuch as he entertains some very original ideas on everything under the sun concerning which he speaks, he must have some very original and interesting views on religion. For the satisfaction of this man permit me to say that Mr. Ford believes, or did once believe, in reincarnation. I have never gone into the subject with him, so I do not know to what extent the belief has taken hold of him. I have heard him say that he has a knowledge of some things with which it seems to him he was born. It comes to him as out of the experience of a former life.

The last question is meant to draw out a

statement as to Henry Ford's ideals, his social theories, his doctrines of human relations, particularly his idea of industrial relations. It comes as a rule from a man who places the emphasis on social rather than individual righteousness, who is interested in the fruits of religion more than in its theological and ecclesiastical roots. He will find the answer to his question scattered here and there throughout these pages, so that I need not restate it here.

To sum it all up, Henry Ford is not a churchman in the sense that he attends any church with regularity, enters into its worship, sacramental or other, is interested in the extension of its work, and contributes toward its support in a manner commensurate with his means. His father was a vestryman in the little Episcopal church in Dearborn. It was in this church that Mr. Ford was baptized and confirmed.

Like many another man, baptized and confirmed in early life, he has not maintained a close contact with organized religion in later years. I cannot conceive of him working contentedly and enthusiastically in any organization, religious or secular, in which he is not the dominating spirit and majority stockholder. If he were to accept the authority and responsibility for the reorganization of the church along lines of efficiency and finance, I have no idea what he would do. But I am sure that whatever he did would go down in ecclesiastical history. Much that is now at the bottom would come to the top, so far as the organization is concerned, and much now at the top would sink into oblivion. We would have the unique spectacle of ecclesiastical conventions meeting annually to devise ways and means for using a surplus, instead of assembling, as at present, for the purpose of working out some plan for meeting the deficit in last year's missionary budget. The clergy might be taken care of by giving them a job six days in the week in the foundry; with the understanding that they preach gratis on the seventh.

I cannot imagine Henry Ford interested in creeds, much less subscribing to one. He is disposed to do his own thinking in matters of religion as in other matters. Theology interests him, but it is not the kind that is found in the seminaries.

He is not an orthodox believer according to the standards of any church that I happen to know.

His religious ideas, as he states them, are somewhat vague. But there is in him something bigger than his ideas, something of a practical nature that is far better than his nebulous theories.

# CHAPTER X

HENRY FORD is a rich man, but he is not a Dives. Dives went to his office every morning, saw Lazarus lying at his gate as he passed out, and did nothing about it. He accepted the beggar as a necessary evil, the outgrowth of a disease in the industrial order for which there was no cure.

It will be recalled that the rich man died and that the beggar died also, and then the tables were turned. It seems that in the hereafter we live on the things we have laid up in the inside of us, not on the things we have piled up outside. This being the case, Dives found himself in bad shape. Spiritually he was in destitute circumstances, and the beggar was rich. The tables, as I have said, were turned, and Dives found himself begging favors of a man who himself had been a beggar.

I am not going to preach a sermon. I have

called to mind the parable of the rich man and Lazarus because it will help me to illustrate some things I want to say regarding Henry Ford in his handling of the ne'er-do-wells in whom in the past he has shown great interest.

Lazarus would not lie unnoticed very long at the gate of Henry Ford. He would not be accepted as a fixed part of the landscape and be permitted to remain there. Something would be done to put him on his feet, something more than giving him a crumb or a coin.

Henry Ford does not believe in beggars; does not believe in the social and economic order that creates them; does not believe in the sentimental charity that encourages beggars to remain in the business of begging.

To the beggar at his gate Henry Ford would say, " Millions for work, but not a cent for charity. You go to the employment office, tell them that I sent you there, and that they are to give you a job. Then go to the doctor's office and have him fix you up. If you would prefer work to begging, you are going to have your chance. What follows will be up to you."

And so, unless the beggar was one of the

professional sort and belonged to the ancient and dishonorable order of voluntary mendicants, he would be given a job — a light job — till he got on his feet, and then he might be transferred to the foundry just to see if he really meant business, really preferred honest work to begging.

If he should develop a yellow streak, that is, ask for a clerical job in the main office, or for a light sitting-down job in the magneto department, he would be back on the street collecting pennies in a tin cup in no time at all. But if he showed that he had the right kind of stuff in him he would be living in a home of his own in a few years and paying an income tax along with the rest of us. If a man is paid six dollars a day in the Ford factory he is expected to earn it and conveyors tuned up to a six-dollar speed leave little to the will of the operator. It's a great system, but it needs careful supervision by human beings.

When the beggar at the gate of Henry Ford is picked up and given a job, his past history is carefully looked into — or there was a time when it would have been. It may be

so now. I cannot say as to that. There was
a time, however, when the beggar hired into
the Ford Motor Company, if he had a wife and
six children in Chicago whom he had deserted
long ago, and toward whose support he had
contributed little or nothing in recent years,
would have been told to bring his family to
Detroit on the next train, or lose his job. Mr.
Ford believes the reconstruction of a man is
not complete so long as he neglects his home.
Money would have been advanced to defray
the expense of bringing the family to Detroit
and later taken in easy payments from the
man's wage. He would have been given as-
sistance in finding a house in which to make
a home for his wife and children. He would
have been encouraged to start a bank account.
In case he proved a little careless in the handling of his money, his pay would have been
turned over to his wife. If the two had showed
a tendency toward extravagance, the profits
of him who had been a beggar would have been
withheld until the lesson of thrift had been
learned. If he were taken ill, a job would
have been given his wife, or a son or daughter,

at six dollars a day until such time as he was able to return to work.

If it were found necessary to send him to a hospital the cost of his care there would have been guaranteed by the company.

If by chance he received an injury while at work he would have received compensation as required by law, and in addition to that a weekly allowance equal at least to half of his wage.

If at any time he showed signs of slipping back into former ways and habits, if he were found to be living in an undesirable neighborhood, he would have been helped to find a house in a better quarter.

If he filled up his house with roomers or boarders, he would have been warned to get rid of them forthwith. His home must be a home. His wife and children must be given a fair chance.

So Henry Ford would have treated Lazarus.

Henry Ford has his faults, but they are not those of Dives. And I cannot think of him as going finally where Dives is. Neither can I quite picture him with Lazarus on the bosom

of Abraham, in view of what he has recently
been saying about Abraham's descendants. It
seems to me the situation would be mutually
embarrassing. I think St. Peter will pass Mr.
Ford at the gate, but following that I fear
that he and Abraham will have to iron out
some personal misunderstandings.

The principles underlying the Ford way of
dealing with his employees, following the establishment of the profit-sharing plan, were
as sound economically as they were humane.
Mr. John R. Lee, through the sociological department, worked out a plan whereby a close,
friendly, man-to-man contact was made between the company and its employees. But the
advisory system, as he established it no longer
exists. It was criticized as paternalistic. It
was not that. It was friendly, fraternal, but
not paternal.

There were employees who objected to it as
subjecting them to humiliating experiences.
They said that it interfered with their personal
liberty and independence. So far as my experience went I found such complaints came
from men whose individual liberties had been

interfered with, but they were such liberties as getting drunk and beating up one's wife, abusing one's family, and wasting one's money.

There were certain men in the city of Detroit, not connected with the Ford Motor Company, who were in a position to judge of the value of this work to Ford employees and to the community as a whole. A judge of the Recorder's Court wrote in regard to the work done by the company for its men:

" In my opinion the community has been a considerable gainer, in that a large number of its citizens have been benefited financially; their standards of living have been raised, and the physical condition of the workers and their families has been improved thereby. I believe their moral condition has also been elevated as a result of the above and also from the necessity for the employees to conduct themselves in a proper manner in order to retain their much prized situations.

" Formerly it was no uncommon occurrence to hear participants in brawls and other offenses testify that they were employees of the Ford Motor Company. Of late it is my impression that I have heard this much less frequently."

From another judge came this:

" I have noticed with sincere pleasure the progress and success of your coöperative plan. Particularly have I been impressed with the system of supervision and investigation which you have established for the purpose of making certain that only the worthy shall participate in the success of the Ford Motor Company. The quality of this service, due in large measure to the painstaking and efficient corps of investigators that you have gathered together, is an object lesson in rational industrial development.

" There would be little social unrest, little industrial discontent, if every employer approached the problem of his relation to his employees, not only with your spirit of fairness and consideration, but also with your system of rational supervision and direction."

The commissioner of police declared that the work done by the company had " decreased in number the cases against your employees," and that the work done by the sociological department " very materially improved the housing conditions in this community, resulting in many thousands of men becoming better and more dependable citizens."

The spirit of coöperation and service was contagious. The doors of executives were open in those days to the humblest of employees who chanced to be in trouble. The desire to help the other fellow spread through the whole organization.

The following story, told by a man who was not in the employ of the company, will serve to illustrate what I know was the effect of the spirit of the company upon its employee in hundreds of instances:

" Beside me in a street car," so the story runs, " there sat a man past fifty years of age. He was a foreigner, and by the badge he wore, I knew he was a Ford employee. A woman entered the car with two small children. Both children were poorly clad. Their stockings were full of holes, their shoes worn. The mother took the smallest of the children on her lap and by doing so exposed two large holes in the knees of the child's stockings. She made attempts to cover these holes, but the little dress was too short to conceal them. Each time the mother tried to hide the holes the old man next to me shifted restlessly in his seat. Presently the woman got off the car and the old man followed her. My curiosity was aroused and I also followed. At the curb he spoke to her. I could not hear what he said, but from gestures made toward the little ones, I gathered that he was interested in them. After talking with the woman for a few minutes he accompanied her to a near-by store. I followed and stood at a distance so that they would not know they were being observed. Stockings, shoes and rubbers were purchased. Also some underwear, and a coat for the smaller child. He left the store with the woman, doffed his cap to her at the door and said ' Good-by.' The woman stood dazed, apparently unable to express the gratitude she felt. I followed the man and spoke to him.

" ' That your daughter? ' I asked.

" ' Who? ' he said.

" ' The woman with the babies.'

" ' No, I don't know her. But did you see

dem poor kids? I got myself four children, and was poor like that. Now I work at Ford's and make good living. When I see dem poor kids it make me think of mine, and I help 'em a little bit.'

" ' What was the woman's name? '

" ' I don't know.'

" ' Where does she live? '

" ' I no ask her.'

" ' What is your name? '

" He looked at me sharply and said, ' You one of dem newspaper men. You write it in de paper. My wife find out, and I catch hell. She no believe me and get jealous. I no give my name.'

" I endeavored to convince him that he was mistaken. It was no use. He hurried away, looking back occasionally to see if I were following him."

There was something in the spirit of those days that called out of men the finest and best in them. One caught a glimpse of a new era in industry. And perhaps the dawn is there — behind the clouds.

# CHAPTER XI

MR. FORD hates the word charity and all that it stands for. He gives generously to friends and employees, but it is in recognition of services rendered. He gives neither a stone nor money to the man who asks bread, but a job.

"No man ever helped another by giving money," he insists.

I have heard him say that the only man on whom he ever bestowed a charity was ruined by it. The amount given in this case was, as I recall it, about seventeen dollars. The investment of that seventeen dollars has saved him millions. Just another example of a wise use of money for which he has become famous.

Mr. Ford has no use for the ordinary channels of charity and philanthropy. Such matters are taken care of by other members of the family. To the Red Cross, the Community

Fund, to people destitute on account of sickness or the infirmity of years, and to many charitable institutions Mrs. Ford and Edsel give generously.

Thousands of people, high and low, great and small, known and unknown, make pilgrimages to Detroit to obtain money from Mr. Ford for every conceivable object under the sun. Many thousands more write letters asking his financial support. It is railroad fare and postage wasted.

A great deal of my time, before I went with the Ford Motor Company and since, has been taken up by people out to get money from Mr. Ford, and who insist that either I put their case up to him, or obtain for them an interview in order that they may plead their own cause. As a matter of curiosity I kept for a time a record of the sums thus sought. The total was close to four million dollars a year.

The requests for money coming into his own office average, so I have been informed, over six million dollars a month.

One request that frequently came under my notice was for a Ford car. The entire output of the factory, it often seemed to me, would hardly meet the demand if every request were to be granted. Charitable, religious and philanthropic institutions and organizations were in need of a Ford runabout or truck — possibly two or three of them, or even forty or fifty of them — right away. Sometimes it was a member of the parish who wanted to "surprise our dear minister" by making him a present of a car. Not infrequently the minister made bold to state his own needs. One bishop wrote asking that two carloads of runabouts be sent to him at once. He had in his diocese a large number of missions and a small number of missionaries; give each of them a runabout and their work could be quadrupled. It was a fine idea. But it was not altogether original. We had been confronted with something like it before. But it required more than one letter to convince the good bishop that if the thought was an inspired one, then inspiration as to the value of Ford runabouts, sedans and trucks in religious, charitable and philanthropic work had become too general for the Ford Motor Company alone to cope with it.

It was necessary to sell a few cars in order to keep going.

Next to a runabout for the parson seemed to be the need for " a bell for our new church." One was almost forced to the conclusion that if every parson had a Ford car, and every church a bell, the pressing religious problems of the country would be at an end.

A man of wealth is confronted by no problem more difficult than that of making a wise use of a portion of his wealth for charitable purposes. To give to ease one's conscience, or to avoid criticism, is not a difficult matter. It can be done by a man who has plenty of money without thought of sacrifice.

Mr. Ford once made a contribution toward the furnishing of a building which I was fitting out for recreational purposes. When he was making out the check for the sum pledged he paused and looking up at me said, " I might as well make this out for a thousand or two more while I am at it." " No," I replied, " the amount you are giving is sufficient. I am not going to expend more than is necessary just because I can get it." " Well," he said, " if you want more, you might as well have it. The gift of money means nothing to me. The only thing I can give you that would mean anything would be my time."

Mr. Ford seldom places a gift in the way of money in a manner that puts it beyond his personal interest and direction. He took over a hospital at a time when it was in financial difficulties. He put millions into it, but before doing so he paid back to others who had previously put money into the institution their contributions in full. "If I am to support that hospital, then I am going to control it," he said to me.

As to the manner of using his money for the benefit of others, Henry Ford has his own ideas. They are not of the conventional sort. Few of his ideas are. His theory that wealth should be amassed in a way that will not create poverty, and so make charity necessary; that the profits of industry are not so much of a private and personal affair as to justify any one man in making even a philanthropic distribution of them; that the proper disposition of such profits is to put them back into indus-

try for the benefit of labor is a theory so near
fundamentally sound that I cannot see much
to justify the criticism that is made of it. Its
weakness, it appears to me, is that it overlooks
the fact that we have not yet reached the industrial millennium in which there is work for
everybody all the time; that accident or old age
may render even a Ford employee helpless in
the struggle for existence; that there are thousands of people in this world now, and thousands more will yet be born, mentally and
physically unequal to do anything that will
give them adequate support. Charity of the
kind that Henry Ford decries, and which we
all decry for that matter, is, as things are, a
necessity, and there seems to be no good reason
why he should not bear his portion of it. His
failure to do so, however, should not blind us
to the great good he is doing in his own way.
We could even afford to have a few more bil-
lionaires like him. But until the millennium ar-
rives we need a few people of means who will
accept our modern organized charity as one
of the necessary evils and give it their support.

In accordance with Mr. Ford's idea as to

the best way to help the other fellow two rules were fundamental in the sociological department of the company. The first was that no problem was to be solved by the use of money when the solution could be reached through work. The second was that no case should be undertaken that could not be put ultimately upon a self-supporting basis.

Thousands of cases of destitution were relieved by giving the head of the family, or some member of it, employment. There was a time when all applicants for employment were looked up before they were hired in, and preference was given to the most needy, to men of large families rather than to men with few dependants, and to married men rather than to single men.

The fact that special consideration was given to old men and cripples brought hundreds of applications from these classes. It was impossible, of course, to take on all who applied, but every effort was made to find places for as many as possible. It was necessary to select special jobs for the old and the physically handicapped. The work must be light and as far removed from danger as possible. I do not recall that a cripple ever received an additional injury while in the employ of the company, and the only instance on record of injury to an old man was the case of one who went to sleep and fell off his chair.

Over one thousand seven hundred cripples were in the employ of the company at the outbreak of the war. In addition to these, some four or five thousand more men, disabled more or less by disease, and who for that reason would be rejected by industry, were on its payroll. After the war the company agreed to take a thousand handicapped men as fast as they came out of hospitals.

Let no one suppose that all this was done as a charity in the ordinary sense of that word. The company prided itself on the fact that it could place these men so that they could earn the wage paid them. Cripples, because of the difficulty they experience in getting a job, as a rule show their appreciation by doing well the work given them. By way of illustration I recall the case of a blind man hired in and put to work. A few days later his foreman brought two men with perfect vision and sound of body to the employment manager. " Here," said the foreman, " take these men and transfer them to some other department. I don't need them. That blind man you gave me the other day is doing their work and his, too, and they are only in his way. And what's more, he keeps singing all the time he is working." He had been a piano tuner. He came to my office and told me his story. He had been able to make enough money to buy food, but friends or family had to help out from time to time in the matter of clothes and room rent. He would like a chance to make his own way in the world. It was given him. And he made good.

Mr. Ford lifted to the level of self-support hundreds of people who otherwise would have been living on the charity of others.

Employees ill and in hospitals, with their savings exhausted, had their hospital bills paid by the company, and in addition to this a weekly allowance, equal to half pay, was given the family. I have known hospital care at the expense of the company to extend in some instances over a period of more than two years. Just so long as the physician stated the man had a chance to recover and return to work, he was regarded as a Ford man, and was taken care of. In all cases where it was possible, however, some member of the family of a sick employee was given work until the employee himself was able to return, and no additional financial aid was given unless absolutely necessary.

Mr. Ford does not believe in old-age pensions. His substitute for them is, as for all other forms of charity, work,— work with better pay for a son or a daughter, or some near relative who will assume the care of the man too old to continue on the job. It was a matter of surprise to me to find how, in the majority of instances, this was a solution better for all concerned than the pension. I have had old men on pension from other industries come into my office begging for work. The pension given them was not sufficient to meet their needs and had had the effect of making the company for which they had formerly worked indifferent to their fate. Here is an instance that illustrates the working out of the Ford plan:

I received a report from one of the branches of the company, that it had in its employ a negro porter past seventy years of age. He was going blind, and, as he worked about the garage, was in danger of being killed or injured. It would be better to pension him and send him home. I asked for a fuller report on the case. I got back a statement that contained little additional information. I then sent a man from the home office who knew what to look for. His report was that the man was past seventy; that he was going blind; that he had a good home practically paid for; that his wife was much younger than her husband and able and willing to work; that the house could accommodate a number of roomers as several rooms were not in use; that there was a stepson about twenty-five years old working in a box factory at twenty-five dollars a week. Here was the solution. Get the son. I asked him how he would like a job at $6 a day on condition that he give a certain weekly amount to his parents. He jumped at the chance. Then we helped fill up the house with a good class of roomers. We went further. We procured the old father a light job as janitor in a small flat a few doors from where he lived. When we got through the income of the family was just about double what it had been. Everybody was at work, and everybody happy. The gift of time, personal interest and a job seemed a very good substitute for a pension.

Mr. Ford's wealth was to the clergy what Noah's incense was to the gods. They swarmed about it like flies. Their requests varied little as to form, and the reason they usually advanced for their being granted was just the one chief reason why they could not be. One was building a church, another a parish house, another a parochial school. "A great many of my parishioners are Ford employees," ran the argument, " and I know Mr. Ford is interested in his people. I am sure he will be glad to help us erect this building." And the answer was, " Mr. Ford is interested in the welfare of his employees. He wants them to have homes of their own, churches and schools. But he thinks that it is better that they should build such for themselves than that he should do it for them. It is for this reason that he pays them a liberal wage and in addition to this shares his profits with them. It is his idea that it is better to spend money through his employees than to spend it on them or for them. Money which others sometimes hold back from their employees and spend on religion, education and charities, he gives to his workmen, believing that it is better for all concerned to make it possible for them to do for themselves. As a rule people appreciate the thing they pay for more than the thing that is given to them — religion included. Which would you prefer, that he cut the wages of your people and give what he saves thereby to you, or that he keep up the wage and let you look to the people for the money with which to carry on your work?" Put that way, they thought the wage better than the gift.

Labor does not take kindly to the man who is spending money in "uplift" work. It prefers to be given the "lift" in wages, and look out for its own uplift.

# THE FORD CHARITIES

There seem to be but three ways by means of which a man of large means can put a portion of his money to philanthropic purposes. He can establish a foundation and leave the disposition of his benevolences to experts. He can personally listen to and investigate every request made, provided he has nothing else to do. Or he can lay down a line of his own and hew to it. This Henry Ford has done. He decries charity. He makes no attempt to conceal that fact. He believes that money should be made to work, and that men should work for money. He insists that anything that can't pay its own way has no right to exist.

# CHAPTER XII

ONE of the most conspicuous, interesting and significant things about the Ford Motor Company is its executive scrap heap. Into it, from time to time, have gone the most capable men of the organization, men of high character and great ability, the value of whose services to the company has been beyond estimate, old and loyal friends of Henry Ford, intimate and trusted business associates for years.

The story of the formation of this scrap heap has never been written, — perhaps never will be. Whatever the causes of its formation, it seems a fair inference to draw that inefficiency was not one of them, in view of the fact that the discard was not made until after the company had attained a phenomenal success.

The character of that scrap heap is such as to lend distinction to the man who is cast upon it. He will find himself in a group of men who are still carrying on in large and successful ways, men whose kindred experiences have given them an open and understanding heart, a sort of a Ford Alumni Association, a postgraduate group who have taken the third degree, doctors of a new philosophy not taught in the universities; a fraternal order, in which there is a buoyant spirit of freedom. Its doors are always open, night and day, and the sentinel stands without, for no one can tell when a new bunch of candidates may arrive.

If you begin to make inquiries concerning the founders of the organization, the original stockholders who financed Mr. Ford in the beginning, you will discover that not one of them is associated with him in the business to-day.

Mr. John S. Gray, stockholder and first president of the company, died while in office. He is the only Ford official of prominence, so far as I know, removed by death. Others have gone in other ways.

The inventor who reaps the reward of his labor is the exception. Mr. Ford is one of the outstanding exceptions. A minority stockholder in the beginning, he gained a controlling interest in a short time through the purchase of the Malcomson stock. Some years later he acquired the stock that remained in the hands of its original holders. He paid liberally for it. For every thousand put into the business he returned millions.

Whether he believed in stock companies or not, at the time the Ford Motor Company was organized, I do not know. In after years he came to regard them with disfavor. Stockholders, in his opinion, as he expressed it, were in danger of becoming " parasites." And so in time the stockholders went.

Mr. James Couzens, original stockholder, a director and an executive in one capacity or another for twelve years.

Mr. John F. Dodge, original stockholder, director and, for a time, vice-president of the company.

Mr. Horace E. Dodge, original stockholder and director.

Mr. John W. Anderson, original stockholder and director.

# THE EXECUTIVE SCRAP HEAP

Mr. Horace H. Rackham, original stockholder and director.

The Gray brothers, Philip, Paul and David, stockholders following the death of their father, and David a director of the company.

Mr. Alexander Y. Malcomson, original stockholder and for two years treasurer of the company, made his bow and exit shortly after the curtain went up on the first act. He has the distinction of heading the line in the great executive trek. He was in reality the organizer and founder of the company. It was the liberal financial backing which he gave, together with the proceeds from the sale of stock which he was chiefly instrumental in placing, that put the organization on its feet in the beginning and made it a going concern.

Mr. James Couzens, for some time Mayor of Detroit, and at present United States Senator from Michigan, left the company in 1915. He had entered it at the time of its organization as bookkeeper, time clerk, purchasing agent, sales manager, and business manager. Down to the time of his resignation he shared in the mind of the public, and justly so, equal honors with Mr. Ford for the phenomenal success of the company. Henry Ford needed in his early years a man capable of managing his business and capitalizing his mechanical genius. Fate sent him James Couzens.

Next to join the silent caravan of executives outward bound were Mr. C. H. Wills and Mr. John R. Lee. I have referred to their contribution to the company elsewhere in these pages.

The next to fold his tent and depart was Mr. Norval A. Hawkins, who had come to the company in 1907 as commercial manager, or in reality as manager of sales. It was he who established and developed to a great extent the sales policies of the company, and laid the foundations of the most thorough, world-wide sales organization in existence.

Then came the exodus of 1920-1921. The list of those who migrated under more or less pressure at that time is a long one. Mention will be made of a few.

Mr. F. L. Klingensmith, at the time he severed his connection with the company, was its vice-president and treasurer. He was also one of its three directors, Mr. Ford and Edsel being the other two. He had entered the organization in 1905 as cashier. At that time there were seven men in the office and seventy in the shop. He rose rapidly, coming in time to be charged with the handling of the finances of the company, determining depositories, the placing and withdrawal of funds, as well as having, in a general managerial capacity, to do with the establishing of the general business policies of the company. Mr. Ford set great value on his services and ability and entrusted to him much of the schooling of Edsel Ford along business lines.

In the first year he was with the company, Mr. Klingensmith also served in the capacity of secretary to Mr. Ford. It was on taking up this work that he spent one whole night opening the accumulated mail of Mr. Ford which filled three waste baskets. Some of this mail had been awaiting action for about two years. In the collection he found company and personal bills, duplicates of which had been paid meantime, and among other things a check for seventy dollars in payment of an old debt.

There is a rumor, which seems to be not without foundation in fact, to the effect that Mr. Ford once tucked a million dollar check in his vest pocket and then proceeded to forget all about it. Mr. Klingensmith says that on one occasion he handed Mr. Ford his monthly salary check and as he did so asked him why he had not deposited the one given him for the previous month. Mr. Ford went through his pockets and turned up the missing check with the remark that he had " forgotten all about it." That was in the days when coal was cheaper. At any rate it must give you a grand and glorious feeling to be able to forget your salary check.

It would appear that attention to details in business was not Mr. Ford's most distinguishing characteristic in those early days. I have heard Mr. Couzens say that he regarded Mr. Ford's ability to delegate the doing of things to some one else as one of the secrets of his success. The three waste baskets full of accumulated mail would seem to bear out in part the correctness of the Senator's observation. Mr. Ford said to me at the time I entered the

124

employ of the company, "My idea of a good executive is that he is a man who never has anything to do." I didn't take that literally, and couldn't see just what he meant. But I understand now.

Mr. William S. Knudson came to the company in 1907 and hit the trail in 1921. He is considered one of the highest authorities in this country on steel stampings and drawings of material. He developed the stamping and drawing operations of the Ford Motor Company in Highland Park. He had charge of mechanical installations in the branches of the company; devised and installed practically all labor-saving equipment for assembling cars; supervised the construction of branch buildings. At the outset of the war he was put in charge of the Eagle Boat operations.

The choice was in recognition of his ability and tireless energy. He had the reputation of getting things done. Knudson was fair and generous in his handling of men. Men liked to work for him. He could drive if necessary, but he seldom found it necessary, for he knew how to lead. They gave him the Eagle Boat job, and he did it. Knudson, like many others, is on the executive scrap heap for no lack of ability and efficiency.

Mr. Charles A. Brownell, " Daddy " Brownell he was affectionately called by all, not — permit me to hasten to say — on account of his age, joined the noble army of martyrs on December 31, 1920. He was hired into the company as advertising manager just before the company ceased to run paid advertising. Following that Mr. Brownell found his relation to Mr. Ford to be very much like that of Aaron to Moses, — spokesman, orator and herald through the columns on the front page of new Ford ideas, policies and achievements. Mr. Brownell has been the interpreter of many cryptic utterances. He also handled very deftly much correspondence that required delicate handling.

In addition to many things of great importance Mr. Brownell handled several side lines. Among these was the job of finding a man able to give us a new translation of the New Testament in the vernacular. Mr. Ford has for a long time wanted a new translation of the

Scriptures — especially of the Christian portion of them. He agrees with St. Peter that Brother Paul wrote many things hard to be understood. Perhaps a new translation would go toward clearing up Paul's thought.

But above all things else Mr. Brownell was himself the evangel of a new gospel, with Henry Ford as all but the deified center of it. No man ever had a greater admiration for Mr. Ford, no one ever had more faith in him. At the Home Office, out in the branch houses, and among the Ford agents, Brownell worked day and night to create the spirit of coöperation, fellowship and good-will. No one did more to build up the morale of the entire organization than he. But his gospel of good-will fell into the hands of the higher critics, and they proved it not only a fond delusion, but a needless overhead expense on production.

Day by day the executive ranks grew thinner. Hartman left. Hubert E. Hartman was the general attorney of the company, and had rendered to it a service of great value, not only in the manner in which he managed its legal relations with the outside world, but in the way he conducted those cases which had to do with the claims of employees against the company for injury and the like. Here a spirit of fairness and liberality marked his action which added as time went on to the company's reputation for dealing on the square with its men.

Besides this, Mr. Hartman, I happen to know, rendered a service to Henry Ford in the Dodge, *Tribune*, and other important trials, perhaps unknown to him, but none the less valuable on that account. Without his contribution in the preparation of these cases and in the collection and preservation of data, the results might have been different.

And there is Mr. Henry Bonner. Mr. Bonner was told to sell his house and stand ready to leave on transfer. He sold his house, but the transfer has not yet come through. He entered the employ of the company about 1914. During his last years with the organization he was in charge of production in the branch houses, and along production lines increased the efficiency of the branches to a point far beyond what it had ever been before.

# THE EXECUTIVE SCRAP HEAP

Still others went at that time, among them eight or ten of the managers of the branches, men who had given years of faithful and efficient service to the company.

Others have gone since, notably the elder Leland and his son, formerly of the Lincoln Motors.

The Ford executive alumni association is always open for business. Wagers on who will be the next to be admitted are forbidden. The only thing sure to happen is the unexpected.

# CHAPTER XIII

## THE FORD INDEBTEDNESS

HENRY FORD has millions in reserve, owes no man a dollar — and is hopelessly in debt.

If the Ford indebtedness were such that it could be met by writing a check it would have been paid in full long ago. But it isn't that kind of an obligation. There are things connected with the formation of his executive scrap heap which leave the impression that Henry Ford is more or less unfamiliar with some of the finer ways of expressing his appreciation of the services rendered him.

It is unfortunate that he has left the impression that the dollar is his favorite standard of measure when he comes to estimate the value of human service. I do not mean to say that he has never paid in any other way. In many instances he has shown friendly and generous consideration beyond the payment of a wage or salary to men in his employ.

# THE FORD INDEBTEDNESS

In other instances men have been rewarded in a way that has left him in their debt. He has paid them liberally, given bonuses, bestowed costly gifts. They started poor with him and ended rich. They began in humble positions and were advanced to places of honor and responsibility and paid princely salaries. If they have gone into the scrap heap later, why should they complain? What more could he or any other man do for them than he has done?

But there are things in human relations which some men prize above money.

There are ways of throwing a man on the scrap heap which leave him with a high regard and a friendly feeling for the man who threw him there. And there are ways which do not. As a rule it is the landing at the end of the fall that hurts. But in the method the Ford Company sometimes resorted to there were painful and unnecessary wounds inflicted by the petard with which a man was hoisted. It wasn't the end of the fall, but the beginning of it that hurt.

A statement regarding Mr. Ford has been put into print and copyrighted to this effect:

"He is as selfish a man as God permits to breathe." I suppose I should give credit to the author of that statement in case I wished to agree to it. But I do not care to agree to it. It does not express the truth as I see it. Mr. Ford is not selfish according to his light. If he knows, as a rule, but one way to pay, it must be admitted that in that way he pays generously. The pity is that he is blind to the value of some higher things. This, as I see it, is the most outstanding and at the same time the most regrettable of the defects in a man in whom there is so much to be admired.

So far as I know, his creditors do not regard the debt due them with anger and resentment, but rather with pity and regret. The operation that removes the scales from a man's eyes may hurt less than the awakening to the fact that his illusions are gone, and he must see things as they are.

The Ford Motor Company is owned and controlled by Henry Ford. He is at present its brains and the originator of its policies.

But the Ford Motor Company as it stands

to-day is not the product of a single mind; far from it. Into its development has gone the thought of some of the keenest minds in the industrial world. Let it be freely granted that Mr. Ford gave to the organization an inventive genius, an insight into the future of the automobile business, a dominating will and personality, yet it must be remembered that there were many things in the game that he did not understand in the beginning.

It seems incredible that he, the modern wizard of finance, ever could have been so impracticable, so uninformed on things concerning which he seems to be so well informed to-day, as to urge the building of a vault at the factory in which to deposit the surplus earnings of the company. He learned a number of things about the game as he went along. By and by he made a sensational touchdown, but there were some rattling good players in the wedge formation that put him over the goal.

James Couzens was, and is, one of the all-American stars in the financial game himself. A masterful man, a little more masterful than Mr. Ford cared to have about; an organizer down to the last detail; a tireless worker who knows how to get work out of others; something of a steam roller when it comes to ironing out difficulties and going through. He made a wonderful captain of the team that finally drove through the line with Henry holding the ball. And when the thing was done he took off his hat and joined with the bleachers in the chorus, " Henry did it."

If any one doubted Couzens' ability before he left the Ford Motor Company his career since leaving should clear up any questions on that point. He is a man with ideas and a will of his own. He is given to forceful expression both in word and deed. It is a statement safely ventured that if he did not originate, he must have greatly modified many of the policies of the company during the time he was with it.

There are men born with too much initiative and independence to live all their lives in a subordinate position, however honorable and lucrative it may be, unless there is given them practically one hundred per cent. freedom and a corresponding amount of responsibility. Neither Mr. Ford nor Mr. Couzens is adapted to the playing of a second fiddle. From what I know of the two men I venture the guess that they did not remain in the same company for the same reason that two locomotives do not run side by side on the same track: not room for both.

Mr. C. H. Wills, a man of recognized ability, a master of shop methods and production with a thorough and practical knowledge of mechanics, an almost uncanny insight into the atomic structure of iron and steel and alloys, the developer of the use of molybdenum, was a sort of fullback on the team, the giver and taker of much punishment. Wherever the line was weakest, he gave it the support of his weight and rush. Wills was an invaluable man to Henry Ford.

Put Mr. Klingensmith and Mr. Hawkins in the line-up where you will — halfbacks possibly — Mr. Klingensmith, in addition to serving in other important positions, selecting and developing men for important positions, filling the gaps in the office organization, handling costs and watching the financial affairs of the company.

# HENRY FORD

Mr. Hawkins sold Ford cars in the days when they had to be sold, before the time when people sat on the front steps waiting for a car to be finished so they could drive it home. Mr. Hawkins organized a sales organization that proved so efficient and got so far ahead of production that it virtually changed the nature of his job. The problem came to be how to keep the people who could not get cars in a good humor till cars could be made for them.

And John R. Lee, the soul of the organization, the champion of the under dog, the friend of the down and out, the man to whom no one ever looked in vain for justice and a square deal. And every time any one handed him a bouquet for his bigness of heart he tossed it over to Henry, and when there was no one around explained to him what it was all about. And Henry kept the flowers.

And there were Brownell, and Hartman, and Bonner, and Knudsen and others in the line-up. A finer, more capable and more loyal group of men never backed a chief. They are not with him now on the upper levels of success, but a number of them were with him when he was making the climb. Granted that he has shown that he no longer needs them, he must admit that much of the momentum that makes the going easier is the stored-up energy of the men who put every ounce of strength in them into the tug of the early days. He may not need them now, but there was a time when he did. He has been a very apt pupil. He is quick to recognize the merit of another man's idea and to appropriate it. But such was the devotion to him of the men about him that they were glad to have him take the credit for all achievements.

It is true that many men who started with him in the early year of the organization developed along with him and shared generously in his material success. It is true that he gave them opportunities to do much greater things than they otherwise ever would have had the opportunity for doing. And it is just as true that they enabled him to achieve a success that he otherwise never would have achieved. It was team work that did it. In all fairness the credit must be distributed. It was a great team, and every member of it deserves great praise.

\* \* \*

At the time the Ford profit-sharing plan went into effect an executive asked Mr. Ford why he did it. The answer was, " Well, let me put it this way: There is nothing left in life, when all is said and done, but good fellow-ship and good-will, is there? Nothing more counts. I would like to see folks who work hard get their share. I would rather give our boys a share of the profits than do anything else."

Here is the conception of the ideal state in industry, — a just return for labor done, good fellowship, and good-will. It is unfortunate that it is not more frequently realized. For "when the shadows lengthen, and the evening comes, and busy world is hushed, and the fever of life is over, and our work is done," then will our wealth be seen to be the friends we have made and held, for " there is nothing left in life, when all is said and done, but good fellowship and good-will, is there?"

# CHAPTER XIV

### INDUSTRIAL SCAVENGERS

WHEN I entered the employ of the Ford Motor Company Mr. Ford had about him the group of great executives mentioned in the preceding chapter. I doubt if there ever came together in any organization a body of men of greater ability, each in his own line or of finer ideals, or broader human sympathies. Certainly no group of men were ever more devoted to the best interests of their company, or were more loyal to their employer.

Loyalty, of course, went for nothing. Mr. Ford derides it; seems to doubt whether such a thing exists between employer and employee. Men work for money. I have always felt it is a pity that he fails to make use of some of these finer things in men; that he does not recognize that there is something which money cannot buy.

In addition to this group of great executives there were hundreds of men in the second and third ranks of the organization who manifested the same enthusiasm in their work and the same loyalty toward their employer.

In every one I met, with a few exceptions to be mentioned later, I found a deep and genuine interest in the well-being of Ford employees. How to humanize the industry to a still greater extent was the subject uppermost on all occasions where Ford men met together, in small groups of employees, in conferences of executives, in meetings of foremen, at banquets, and managers' conventions. One felt one's self to be a part of a great experiment in applied Christianity in industry. The spirit of service, helpfulness and coöperation permeated practically the whole organization. The world was told that in the Ford Motor Company it had an example of what could be achieved through a just, generous and humane handling of labor. Here was a corporation with a soul.

But there are men in every organization to whom the higher things in life make no appeal.

# INDUSTRIAL SCAVENGERS

There were some men of this kind in the employ of Henry Ford. They never understood the better, finer policies of the company and never ceased to ridicule, criticize and misrepresent the efforts put forth to improve the human relations within the industry. To them the morale of the organization meant nothing. They also flouted loyalty on the part of employees as being of no value. They stoutly held that men worked for two reasons — their wage, and the fear of losing their jobs.

The humane treatment of employees, according to these men, would lead to the weakening of the authority of the " boss," and to the breaking down of discipline in the shop. To them the sole end of industry was production and profits, and the one sure way of getting these things out of labor was to curse it, threaten it, drive it, insult it, humiliate it, and discharge it on the slightest provocation; in short — to use a phrase much on the lips of such men — "put the fear of God into labor." And they were always thinking of themselves as the little gods who were to be feared.

There were not many men of this sort in the

Ford Company when I entered it. But the few who were there seemed to be in a closer and more confidential relation to Mr. Ford than those who stood for the better things, and this in spite of the fact that for the time being he seemed heartily in favor of the humane policies then in force.

Why he made familiars of men of this class was a profound mystery to those of us who saw only the other side — the nobler and better side — of him. In an article by Mr. W. P. Wilson, which appeared some time ago in the *World's Work,* entitled "An Intimate Study of Lloyd George," there is to be found this paragraph:

"Asked why he (Lloyd George) sometimes chooses such curious friends, he would probably answer that you can not govern mankind by idealists. 'You need scavengers to clean your streets,' is one of his most interesting maxims. Lloyd George has always been particularly careful to select skillful scavengers. They are in attendance on him everywhere, loyally doing the dirty work of national housekeeping. He is as much amused with them as he is with any other menagerie. He loves the unusual and grotesque. . . . No great man ever suffered fools more gladly. And the fools know it. . . . Lloyd George is the apotheosis of the common man. He has the common man's contempt for theory, the common man's contact with facts."

Henry Ford is also particularly careful to select skillful scavengers on occasion when he deems their services necessary. They seem to furnish him with the unusual and the grotesque at which he does not frown, if he does not smile. If the work of certain clerks in the shop is not wanted, why tell them so? Smash their desks. That is quite unusual, deliciously grotesque, and very amusing. A man who ventures to wear a white collar in a shop deserves to have his life made a burden. Expensive tools of skilled workmen are scattered over the floors. Foolish? Insulting? Humiliating? Not at all. It takes the conceit out of the man who prides himself on his work. It prevents him getting into a " cozy corner " and admiring himself over-much.

It is curious that both Lloyd George and

Henry Ford should seem to have lost faith in their early idealism, Lloyd George having discovered that you cannot govern an empire, and Henry Ford discovering that you cannot govern a factory, by idealists. Perhaps they are right. I am simply recording the fact as an interesting one. Still some of us will cling to the theory that men respond more generously to good treatment than to harsh, that men can be led to work up to their fullest capacity, and that all are better for being led than driven.

It became evident as time went on that either the men who stood for the better things in the organization, or the scavengers, must go. The ideals and policies announced in 1914-1915 became increasingly difficult of enforcement. Rules for the handling of employees were bent and frequently broken. Then came the depression of 1920. Curtailment in production was followed by curtailment of construction work. The wheels stopped. So also the incoming stream of gold. Staggering obligations were ahead. Men were let out from necessity. That in itself merits no criticism.

# INDUSTRIAL SCAVENGERS

It was not what was done, but the manner in so many instances in which men were discharged.

If there is any act in industry that should be done with the utmost consideration, it is the act of discharge, especially in the time of crisis.

It is sufficiently painful and humiliating to be brought face to face with unemployment and all that follows — loss of income and of savings, accumulation of debts, eviction and hunger — without being kicked like a dog into it.

Discharge and reorganization are not necessarily dirty work. It is the last sort of work in the world to be placed in the hands of the industrial scavengers. Unfortunately there are employers who think otherwise. In times like the present, when there are more men than jobs, when often men are driven in production to the point of exhaustion, the scavenger, whose delight is in the brutal methods that prevailed in the days of slavery, is having his day in many an industry.

It does not require many men of this sort to

destroy a company's reputation for just dealing, cloud its good name, and convert the goodwill of labor and the general public into silent, but effective opposition. The law of compensation works in the handling of men in industry, as in all other things. In the end we reap what we sow.

# CHAPTER XV

IT was toward the close of the year 1915 that I gave up the deanship of St. Paul's Cathedral, Detroit, and took charge of the Sociological department of the Ford Motor Company. I continued in the employ of the company for a period of a little more than five years.

The sociological department — later known as the educational department — had been organized early in the year 1914, at the time the Ford profit-sharing plan, with its five-dollars-a-day minimum pay went into effect. To Mr. John R. Lee, who organized the department and conducted its work for the first two years of its existence, credit is due, more than to any other one man, for devising those unique humane policies which attracted world-wide attention, and which gave a practical and helpful

147

direction to the philanthropic impulses of Mr. Ford. There is in Mr. Lee a rare combination of qualities which were needed at the time in the development of the personnel work of the company.

Mr. Ford has a way of making great things possible, of opening the door of opportunity for others. And fortunately for him, he has been able in the past to gather about him men who have been able to seize upon these opportunities and to use them in a way that has reflected great credit upon him and upon themselves. If it had not been for Mr. Lee, I am inclined to think that the sociological work of the Ford Motor Company would have taken its course along lower and conventional lines. He is a man of ideas and ideals. He has a keen sense of justice and a sympathy with men in trouble that leads to an understanding of their problems. He has an unbounded faith in men, particularly in the " down and outs," without which no man can do constructive human work. Under his guidance the department put a soul into the company and gave intelligent direction to the generous thought and will of Mr.

Ford and Mr. Couzens toward their employees. Mr. Lee must be credited with being one of the makers of the Ford Motor Company on its human side.

A few days after the profit-sharing plan went into effect I called upon Mr. Ford at his request. We sat in his office talking and looking out on a great throng of men gathered in the street below, drawn there in the hope that they might be able to obtain employment at the hitherto unheard-of rate of pay. On many previous occasions he had talked over with me his desire to share in some practical manner his prosperity with his employees. As we sat there that morning he spoke at length of his plans and purposes and of the motives back of them. I asked him why he had fixed upon five dollars as the minimum pay for unskilled labor. His reply was, " Because that is about the least a man with a family can live on in these days. We have been looking into the housing and home conditions of our employees and we find that the skilled man is able to provide for his family, not only the necessities, but some of the luxuries of life. He is able to educate his children, to rear them in a decent home in a desirable neighborhood. But with the unskilled man it is different. He's not getting enough. He isn't getting all that's coming to him. And we must not forget that he is just as necessary to industry as the skilled man. Take the sweeper out of the shop and it would become in a short time an unfit place in which to work. We can't get along without him. And we have no right to take advantage of him because he must sell his labor in an open market. We must not pay him a wage on which he cannot possibly maintain himself and his family under proper physical and moral conditions just because he is not in a position to demand more."

"But suppose the earnings of a business are so small that it cannot afford to pay that which, in your opinion, is a living wage; what then?" I asked.

"Then there is something wrong with the man who is trying to run the business. He may be honest. He may mean to do the square thing. But clearly he isn't competent to conduct a business for himself, for a man who cannot make a business pay a living wage to his employees has no right to be in business. He should be working for some one who knows how to do things. On the other hand, a man who can pay a living wage and refuses to do so is simply storing up trouble for himself and others. By underpaying men we are bringing on a generation of children undernourished and underdeveloped morally as well as physically; we are breeding a generation of workingmen weak in body and in mind, and for that reason bound to prove inefficient when they come to take their places in industry. Industry will, therefore, pay the bill in the end. In my opinion it is better to pay as we go along and save the interest on the bill, to say nothing of being human in our industrial relations. For this reason we have arranged to distribute a fair portion of the profits of the company in such a way that the bulk of them will go to the man who needs them most."

"But some people are saying," I suggested, "that this sudden increase in pay, amounting in thousands of instances to the doubling of a man's income, is going to ruin more men

than it will make. Unaccustomed to so much
money many a man will waste it — spend it
in foolish and harmful ways."

" We are not afraid of that," he replied.
" In the first place we are planning to help
the man who is weak and needs our help. We
are going to go along with him in a friendly
way until he is able to walk alone. And more
than that, I believe that the great majority of
men may be trusted to do the right thing if
given the chance. There are thousands of men
out there in the shop who are not living as they
should. Their homes are crowded and insani-
tary. Wives are going out to work because
their husbands are unable to earn enough to
support the family. They fill up their homes
with roomers and boarders in order to help
swell the income. It's all wrong — all wrong.
It's especially bad for the children. They are
neglected from necessity. Now, these people
are not living in this manner as a matter of
choice. Give them a decent income and they
will live decently — will be glad to do so.
What they need is the opportunity to do better,
and some one to take a little personal interest

in them — some one who will show that he has faith in them."

He was silent for a moment and sat gazing at the crowd in the street below. Then he said, " I'll tell you what I'll do. Blindfold me and lead me down there into the street and let me lay my hands by chance on the most shiftless and worthless fellow in the crowd and I'll bring him in here, give him a job with a wage that offers him some hope for the future, some prospect of living a decent, comfortable and self-respecting life, and I'll guarantee that I'll make a man out of him. All that man needs is an opportunity that has some hope in it, some promise for the years to come."

Two years later I was asked to take charge of the sociological department. With practically unlimited means and opportunities for carrying on the work at my disposal, and with Mr. Ford deeply interested in it, as he was at that time, it seemed to me an unusual chance for service in a field into which I had always longed to enter, but into which I had never been permitted to go.

" We want to make men in this factory as

well as automobiles," is the way Mr. Ford put the matter to me at that time. " This company has outlived its usefulness as a money-making concern, unless we can do some good with the money. I do not believe in charity, but I do believe in the regenerating power of work in men's lives, when the work they do is given a just return. I believe that the only charity worth while is the kind that helps a man to help himself. And I believe that I can do the world no greater service than to create more work for more men at larger pay. I can foresee the time when we will have a hundred thousand men — and more — employed in this industry, and I want the whole organization dominated by a just, generous and humane policy."

Such were some of the ideas and ideals of Henry Ford in the years 1914-1915. In accepting the position he offered me I did not think of myself as entering the employ of an impersonal thing called a corporation, but as working with a man whom I had known for many years and for whom I had an unbounded admiration.

# LIGHTS

I resigned from the Ford Motor Company in 1921. The old group of executives, who at times set justice and humanity above profits and production, were gone. With them, so it seemed to me, had gone an era of coöperation and good-will in the company. There came to the front men whose theory was that men are more profitable to an industry when driven than led, that fear is a greater incentive to work than loyalty.

The old, humane policies were still professed, but the new influence which had gained the ascendency made impossible, so far as I was concerned, an honest and consistent application of those policies. " Loyalty and good-will on the part of the employees toward the company were discounted. Men worked for money," I was informed. " Pay them well, and then see to it that you get your money's worth out of them," seemed to be the new policy of the company.

Perhaps Mr. Ford should be permitted to state for himself a view which seems in conflict with the doctrine of " fellowship and good-will," and the slogan, " Help the other fellow," which had prevailed for a number of years as the expression of human policy of the company. In a recent authorized statement he says:

" Some organizations use up so much energy and time maintaining a feeling of harmony that they have no force left to work for the object for which the organization was created. The organization is secondary to the object. The only harmonious organization that is worth anything is an organization in which all the members are bent on the one main purpose —not to get along with itself, but to get along toward the objective. A common purpose, honestly believed in, sincerely desired — that is the great harmonizing principle.

" I pity the poor fellow who is so soft and flabby that he must always have ' an atmosphere of good feeling ' around him before he can do his work. There are such men. They produce with a sort of hothouse fervor while they are being coddled, but the moment the atmosphere chills and becomes critical they become helpless. And in the end, unless they obtain enough mental and moral hardiness to lift them out of their soft reliance on ' feeling,' they are failures. Not only are they business failures; they are character failures also; it is as if their bones never attained a sufficient degree of hardness to enable them to stand on their own feet. There is altogether too much reliance on good feeling in our business organizations. People have too great a fondness for working with the people they like. In the end it spoils a good many valuable qualities.

" Do not misunderstand me when I use the term ' good feeling.' I mean that habit of making one's personal likes and dislikes the sole standard of judgment. Suppose you do not like a man. Is that anything against him? It may be something against you. What have your likes or dislikes to do with facts? Every man of common sense knows that there are men whom he dislikes, who are really more capable than he is himself." [1]

Once in a while I found a man in the office or the shop of the kind Mr. Ford describes. He was eternally seeking a transfer because he

[1] " My Life and Work," H. Ford and S. Crowther. Doubleday, Page and Company, 1922.

did not personally like some one under whom, or with whom he had to work. He must breathe the atmosphere of " good feeling " found only in mutual admiration societies, or cease to function. The fault was in the man, not in the organization. Full of personal prejudices, he created wherever he went the very atmosphere of which he complained. The average man is not dependent on " good feeling " of the kind described, but he does require the atmosphere of good-will to bring out the best in him. The foreman or executive who arouses in men the spirit of hate and antagonism through unjust and inhuman treatment is calling out that which is not only injurious to his own organization, but is a menace to industry as a whole.

It may be that more can be gotten out of men who are driven than out of men who are led. It may be that hate and fear are stronger incentives to work than good-will and loyalty. But I don't believe it. For the time being; yes, possibly. But in the end what?, For the violation of certain laws we may never be brought into a court of justice. But we pay the penalty in the end, just the same. There are laws which men do not make and which do not depend on men for their enforcement.

# CHAPTER XVI

A STILL picture of Henry Ford is impossible, for the simple reason that there is something in him that is never still. He thinks quickly and he acts quickly, and he is always thinking and acting. His normal state seems to be that of mental agitation, and it is an agitation that is contagious. In his presence no one is ever entirely at his ease; at least that is true of his employees. You come to feel certain of but one thing, and this is that with any work which he has to do, the unexpected is bound to happen. There is about him the fascination of an unlimited uncertainty. No living being knows what he is likely to say or do next.

The outward man reveals what is within. The ever-changing expression of his face, the constant play upon it of lights and shadows reflecting his rapidly changing thoughts and moods are the subject of remark on the part of those who see Mr. Ford daily.

Photographers complain that he is "hard to get." There are snapshots of him a-plenty. Each looks as he looks at times. But no one of them reveals him as he is. No satisfactory photograph of him, so far as I know, has ever been taken. No life-like portrait of him has ever been painted, that I have seen, and I venture to say none revealing the inward man ever will be. There is something in his face too elusive either for camera or brush, just as there is something deep within him so complex, so contradictory, so elusive as to defy description. It is a face that reveals an extraordinary alertness rather than depth of thought. Poise and repose are not present to any marked degree.

The face of Henry Ford is the mirror of his mind. One is as difficult to photograph as the other. Mental snapshots there are of him in abundance, but anything approaching a true mental portrait of him has never yet been made. Henry Ford to be known must be seen in action, not once or twice, but many times. The only mental picture of him possible is a moving mental picture, a series of impressions, of sketches made on the spot, revealing him swayed, as he is, by various and conflicting thoughts and emotions.

It has been my privilege to observe him in his widely differing moods, to study him under a variety of circumstances, and to discuss with him many things. In addition to this I know many of his executives — past and present — and have talked over with them often and at length the impressions he has made on them, and in this way I have had opportunity to verify, or correct my own impressions.

I have seen Henry Ford at work and at play. I have been with him on occasions when he was facing the ridicule of the world, and again when he was receiving its applause.

But in spite of a long and fairly intimate acquaintance with him, I have not one mental picture of him, as I have already intimated, of which I can say, " This is as he is, or as I know him." There are in him lights so high and shadows so deep that I cannot get the whole of him in proper focus at the same time.

Pilgrimages to Highland Park and Dearborn are made by people from all parts of the world. They come to learn the truth about Henry Ford. Some of them will tell you that they are bent on making the one true pen sketch of a man whose name is associated in their minds with that of Lincoln and,— but respect for the one and reverence for the Other forbids the mentioning in this connection of the second name. I have met in the past many of these would-be painters of Henry Ford. Now and then one makes his way to my door even yet. I know the itinerary that was marked out for them on their arrival. I know the offices through which they were routed. I am familiar with the material that was given them. Now and then a favored individual was given an interview with Mr. Ford himself. With rapt attention he heard him express his ideas, discuss his policies, and unfold his plans, and then he went away and made a picture — a mosaic of second-hand mental impressions and of carefully selected facts. I have never seen one of these pictures in which the lights and shadows were true to life. Some were almost all light, and others were nearly all shadow, depending somewhat, I suppose, on the prejudices and the point of view of the one making the sketch.

Ford executives — in and out — know that no man can know Henry Ford who has not lived for some time in his industrial family; that no true impression of him can be obtained from one or more formal or informal interviews with him.

As in every other man, there is in Henry Ford the mingling of opposing elements. In him, however, the contrast between these elements is more pronounced than in the average man. Phenomenal strength of mind in one direction is offset by lamentable weakness in another. Astounding knowledge of and insight into business affairs along certain lines stand out against a boasted ignorance in other matters. Sensational achievements are mingled with equally sensational failures. Faith in his employees and, at times, unlimited generosity toward them are clouded on occasion by what seems to be an utter indifference to the fate and feelings of men in his employ. There seems to be no middle ground in his make-up.

# SHADOWS

There is no unifying spirit in the warring elements of his nature. There is no line discernible, that I have ever been able to detect, that marks the resultant of the opposing forces within him, and to which one may point and say, " This is the general trend of his life."

He has in him the mental and moral qualities of a great character, if only they were properly blended. He is neither erratic nor unbalanced, as some would have us believe. The true explanation of him seems to me to be this: his mind has never been organized (due, perhaps, in large part to the absence of early educational influences) and his moral qualities and impulses, among which are to be found some of the highest and noblest I have ever known grouped in any one man, have never been compounded and blended into a stable, unified character. One of the most extraordinary and outstanding facts in regard to him, the inexplicable and ironical contradiction, is that a genius in the use of methods for the assembly of the parts of a machine, he has failed to appreciate the supreme importance of the proper assembly, adjustment and balance of the parts of the mental and moral machine within himself. He has in him the makings of a great man, the parts lying about in more or less disorder. If only Henry Ford were properly assembled! If only he would do in himself that which he has done in his factory!

There are times when I felt that the balance had been struck, when the warring elements in his nature had come finally to rest, the blend hoped for had been attained, and then the fires slumbering in him have broken forth with volcanic suddenness and fury, and regrettable qualities have come to the surface. In character he persists in remaining a mixture which defies classification, and in that respect at least, resembles a certain order of genius.

In spite of these displays of contradictory sides of character one never ceases to hope that some day, under heat and pressure of some kind, these mental and moral forces will be fused and blended into one great personality. If only the proper mixture were to be attained and held. If only the scales would cease their endless oscillation, Henry Ford would easily stand out as one of the great characters of this and all time.

It was this which I have just written that I had in mind when I said that I had no one mental picture of him of which I can say, " This is as he is, or as he appears to me." I find that all I can do is to record a series of impressions which he has made upon me, impressions which have varied greatly from time to time, and from which it is impossible for me to develop a simple, satisfactory, composite picture.

I am aware that our impressions of men are after all just impressions. A man is what he is, and not necessarily what others think him to be. Still, when a man leaves practically the same impression on all who have long and intimate relations with him, it is fair to assume that there is something within him which bears a close resemblance to the impression he has made.

# CHAPTER XVII

## AN ELUSIVE PERSONALITY

HENRY FORD possesses the most elusive personality of any man I have ever known.

My observation has been that people who are sure that they know all about him are those who have very slight acquaintance with him, whose contact with him has been very superficial, or who have come in contact with him not at all, but rest their judgment of him on what is said by others whose first-hand knowledge is as limited as their own. He has another guess coming who imagines that Henry Ford is a sort of unsophisticated farm and shop product — just a country boy grown to man's size — and altogether so frank and honest that his very simplicity is his defense; that the mind that created the Ford car is as devoid of puzzling parts and intricate machinery as the car itself.

# AN ELUSIVE PERSONALITY

It may be that the difficulty that one experiences in arriving at a true understanding of Mr. Ford is due to the fact that he deliberately draws a herring across the trail in case he finds a man getting too close to him. "You know me too well," he once said to a man who had been intimately associated with him for years; "hereafter I am going to see to it that no man comes to know me as intimately as you do." But personality is something that cannot be hidden at will. The very attempt to conceal it is in itself a revelation.

It is not due to any conscious effort on the part of Mr. Ford to prevent a close-up study of himself that makes him difficult of understanding.

The baffling thing in him is the puzzling mixture of opposing natures.

There rages in him an endless conflict between ideals, emotions and impulses as unlike as day and night, — a conflict that at times makes one feel that two personalities are striving within him for mastery, with neither able to win a final decision over the other.

These variations in mental moods and attitudes are generally accompanied by outward changes in physical appearance. To-day he stands erect, lithe, agile, full of life, happy as a child, and filled with the child spirit of play. Out of his eyes there looks the soul of a genius, a dreamer, an idealist, — a soul that is affable, gentle, kindly, and generous to a fault. But to-morrow he may be the opposite. He will have the appearance of a man shrunken by long illness. The shoulders droop, and there is a forward slant to the body when he walks as when a man is moving forward on his toes. His face is deeply lined, and the lines are not such as go to make up a kindly, open countenance. The affable, gentle manner has disappeared. There is a light in the eye that reveals a fire burning within altogether unlike that which burned there yesterday. He has the appearance of a man utterly wearied and exhausted, and yet driven on by a relentless and tireless spirit. Back of an apparent physical frailty there evidently lies concealed a boundless supply of nervous energy.

His executives came to recognize an outward physical change, such as I have just described, with its corresponding mental attitude, as the signal of a storm,— sudden and terrible as those which break over the tropics. As a rule, not many days would elapse before the organization would be in the throes of one of its periodical convulsions. And only a Ford man who has gone through them has any idea what these convulsions are like. Old policies are swept away. New policies are set up. Departments are turned inside out and upside down, or altogether done away with. Men are transferred by the score, sometimes by the hundreds. Desks are removed on one or two occasions with an ax. The men who worked at them return to find them gone, and possibly their jobs gone also. Men are discharged without warning, and no reason is given them in response to their inquiry.

While the storm is on there is little to do but to watch it and keep out of the way of the lightning.

When the blow was over, then those of us whose duty it was, would get out the ambulance and pick up the injured. Men discharged or temporarily displaced were quietly put back to work; others who had been hastily transferred to jobs unsuited to them slipped into jobs for which they were fitted. And sometimes departments which had been demolished were rebuilt in whole or in part because the work they were doing was essential to the life of the organization.

There was much needless suffering at such times. The morale of the organization was weakened. Faith in its policies of justice and fair play was shaken as well.

Of course Mr. Ford's hand did not directly appear in these upheavals. Down in the ranks of his employees the belief prevailed that he knew nothing of what was going on (for a long time I held to this belief myself, being forced to surrender it with great reluctance) but that the trouble was due to the " roughneck " methods of two or three of his lieutenants. The appeal of Ford employees at such times, seeking some redress for the injustice done them, was always to the spirit of fair play for which they believed Mr. Ford stood. " He, of course, does not know the way we have been handled," was always the argument of the man seeking reinstatement or transfer after the storm. " We know that he would not sanction the treatment accorded us." But he did know in general what was going on, and individual cases in which it seemed to me flagrant injustice had been done were called to his attention.

A case in point. There was a certain man who had been in the employ of the company for a number of years. He was a trained man and held a responsible position. His task was a colossal one and greatly complicated by conditions which arose during the war. He was discharged. He asked for reasons for his discharge, but was given an evasive answer. He came to me broken up and in tears over the matter. I brought the case to Mr. Ford's attention. I told him that the manner of the man's discharge not only deprived him of his job, but robbed him unjustly of his reputation. It impaired his standing in his profession. The treatment was neither just nor humane. Mr. Ford said to me, " If you think he has not been given a square deal, go and get him, bring him back and we will give him a job."

Before acting in accordance with these instructions I made a thorough investigation of the case. I interviewed officials who were in daily contact with the man and his work. I questioned foremen and sub-foremen who had worked under him. I could find nothing to justify the action taken. I then told Mr. Ford I was ready to act in the case. He asked me if after investigating the matter I still believed the man had not had a square deal. I told him I was more convinced of that fact than ever. "Very well," he said, "get him and we will put him back." Within an hour he told me that a certain executive wished to talk with me regarding this case. I went to that man's office and listened to a number of charges against the discharged man which the facts, as I had gathered them from the man's superior, his equals, and the men under his direction, did not bear out. I told this executive that I thought he had acted most unfairly in the discharge of this man. "How do you know I did it?" he shot back. "Maybe you are barking up the wrong tree. How do you know the Chief did not do it?" I answered that I did not believe the Chief would be capable of doing such a thing. While we were in the midst of a heated discussion Mr. Ford came into the office. He listened to what we were saying for a few minutes and then turning to me said, " I did it. I discharged that man, and what is more, he is not coming back." This within an hour after he had said for the second time that he would be taken back.

" What have you got to say now? " said the official. " I told you that you were barking up the wrong tree."

" I have to say," I replied, " just what I have said before. The discharge was not merited, and the manner in which it was done was neither courteous nor fair."

Mr. Ford then said, " Bring the man down to my office in the morning and we will go over the whole matter with him."

I did as requested. Mr. Ford failed to keep the appointment. That was the end of the case. And it was the beginning, for me, of an awakening to things of which I wish I could have remained in ignorance.

Frequently a man slated to go was not told

to go. He was nagged; his department was interfered with by others under instruction to do so; his work was taken away from him. In one instance more than eighty men in one department went home one evening with no intimation whatever that they were through. They came to work the next morning to find their desks and chairs taken from the room in which they worked. They were left to find out as best they could that they had been fired.

The request to be permitted to tell men in a decent, gentlemanly manner that the company no longer required their services was met with refusal. The way preferred and chosen was to " bump 'em off "; " rag 'em till they go." Why? That is a question to which, in the wildest flights of my imagination, I have been able to find no answer. Perhaps it is due to the theory held that loyalty is " bunk," and good-will is of no value anyhow.

A factory is not a church. I am well aware of that. There come critical times in business when sentiment must be put to one side. But there never comes a time when it is necessary to treat human beings other than as such.

# AN ELUSIVE PERSONALITY

A major operation may be necessary to save the life of an industry, but just because there must be a major operation is no reason why you should engage the services of a butcher and not a surgeon.

And let me repeat it: it was never to the operation that I objected, but to the brutal and unnecessary butchery that went with it.

The general who gives the order does not see the individual casualties which follow. But he does give the order, and he does know — or should know — whether or not the men to whom he entrusts the execution of his orders are considerate of the individual in the accomplishment of the end sought.

It is as unnecessary, as it is unfortunate, that an employer of labor should keep in power men who in the treatment of employees believe in the slogan, " Treat 'em rough." It is still more unfortunate that such men, instead of meeting reproof, are advanced and rewarded because of their apparent value in times when disagreeable work is to be done. But the responsibility for the action of such men rests squarely upon the shoulders of their employers, no matter what their personally professed humanitarian policies or theories may be.

# CHAPTER XVIII

## EDSEL FORD

"THERE is one job in this war I do not want and will not take, and that is the job of a rich man's son."

It was Edsel Ford who made this statement to me and the circumstances which called it forth, together with the tone of sincerity and righteous indignation in which it was uttered, left upon my mind an indelible impression, — the impression that I was in the presence of a man whose character, patriotism, courage and ideals were such as to make the martyrdom which he was suffering at the time one of the most unjust and barbarous cruelties inflicted during the war. And it was a martyrdom, as we knew who saw him day after day going steadily and silently about his work, facing the great problems and shouldering the enormous responsibilities involved in changing over from

179

a peace basis to a one hundred per cent. war basis one of the largest industries in the country.

It was at the time that Edsel Ford was being scored by his critics for not offering himself for military service that I had a talk with him concerning the matter during which he made the statement above quoted. Before recording more fully what passed between us at that time, there are one or two things which ought to be stated, which will go a long way toward explaining Edsel Ford's action at that time.

Edsel Ford was a mere boy in his 'teens when his father began to train him for the management of the business which sooner or later would devolve upon him. It was arranged that the boy should acquire by actual experience a thorough, practical knowledge of both office and shop. It was Mr. Ford's purpose to share his responsibilities with his son as fast as the latter was able to assume them.

Edsel Ford did not go to college. It is my impression that he did not care to do so. I know his father was not eager for him to have a university training. The son remained at home and followed to the letter his father's plans in regard to his practical education. He was a boy clean in mind and habits, and of exceptional strength of character. Few young men have been as little influenced by prospective millions as he.

Two or three things happened during the war which for a time had a decided effect on Henry Ford's interest in and attitude toward his business in Highland Park.

First of all, with the outbreak of the war in 1914, he became an ardent pacifist, and devoted a great deal of his time to propaganda and measures of one kind and another which he honestly and sincerely believed at the time would tend to shorten that conflict. He was so absorbed in his pacifist undertakings — the Peace Ship, for example — that his mind was more or less withdrawn from his business.

Another matter that tended to lessen his interest in the Highland Park plant was the development of a farm tractor at the Dearborn shops. I think the tractor, because of its utility, appealed to him more than the car.

Then came the building of the Rouge plant
which ultimately involved him in litigation
with some of the stockholders of his company.
This litigation seemed to arouse in him at times
a feeling of antagonism toward the plant at
Highland Park, so much so that he seemed on
the point of starting the manufacture of another car; did announce, if my memory serves
me rightly, that he had the establishment of another plant and the building of another car in
mind.   At any rate, his interest in affairs at
Highland Park, to all appearances, were on the
wane.   He came infrequently to his office.   He
was more than ordinarily difficult to reach.
The result was that to Edsel Ford the executives of the company turned more and more for
important decisions in the shaping or approval
of policies affecting the conduct of the business.
Back of the son was the father, of course, and
doubtless no action of great importance was
taken without the father's knowledge and advice, but the fact remains that the approach to
the father for a long time was, as a rule,
through the son.   In short, the son came to be
regarded as the active head of the business and

absolutely indispensable to the conduct of it under the circumstances. This was the situation in the Ford Motor Company when this country entered the war.

I happened to be one of the men who went before the draft board in the case of Edsel Ford and stated that it was my conviction that he was indispensable to the successful conduct of the war work being done in the Highland Park plant. What I said then I — together with all other executives familiar with the situation — believed to be the absolute truth. I am of the same opinion still.

But let us put this all to one side. Opinions may differ as to its value and bearing on the case. I will pass to something that reveals the attitude of Edsel Ford toward military service, and about which there can be no two opinions.

In conversation with Edsel Ford at the time that the criticism of his action was at its height, I said to him, "We who know the circumstances believe that you are needed here; that you can render a more valuable service to your country in directing the war work being done here in this plant than in any other capacity.

But, as you know, the public is ignorant of the circumstances requiring your presence here. Because of this you are being misunderstood and subjected to criticism and insult. I believe that there is a way out which will make it possible for you to enter the service and at the same time keep in close touch with this business. I believe that if all the facts were put before the authorities in Washington you would be given an appointment in connection with the military service in this district that would permit of your keeping in close touch with affairs here. We would still have you within reach to advise us in matters of importance."

His answer was, " The matter you propose has already been suggested to me. I have been assured that such an appointment could be secured for me. But I refuse absolutely to let any one take such action in my behalf. I honestly believe that I can render my best and most valuable service here. But if not here in connection with this business — then in France. I want no stay-at-home appointment. I will accept none. I do not want to don a uniform with the assurance that I will be expected to do nothing but sit in a swivel chair. There is one job in this war I do not want and will not take, and that is the job of a rich man's son. If the authorities, in whose hands my case is resting, feel that I am mistaken in my belief that I can render my best service here, then I would prefer the trenches to a swivel chair."

And this was the man at whom were being hurled the epithets of " coward," " pacifist " and " slacker." No man labored harder and more conscientiously, and rendered a more valuable and patriotic service to his country than he.

Minds aflame with what they call patriotism sometimes work in peculiar ways. One of the men connected with certain war activities in the city of Detroit, and one who had been most vehement in his denunciation of Edsel Ford, asked me through a second party to furnish him with a man from my department qualified to do a certain work in connection with his office. I sent word to him that I had a man specially fitted to do the work he wanted done; that he was a cripple and so not able for active service, but specially anxious to do his bit; that his present salary was so much, and that I thought he would prove himself worth that amount and more to him. His answer was — this noisy critic of Edsel Ford — " I don't want your man if I have to pay him a salary. There are plenty of rich men's sons in this town who can afford to do this work for nothing, and as it will carry exemption from military duty, they would jump at the job." Comment is unnecessary, and if couched in suitable language might not be considered fit to print.

Toward the close of the year 1918 I sat with a committee in Edsel Ford's office working out a bonus system which meant the distribution among the employees on January 1st of the following year of a large sum of money, approximately ten millions of dollars. In the midst of the conference the superintendent of the shop — who chanced to be one of the committee — was called out of the room. He returned in a few minutes looking very grave. " We have just been notified," he said, " that on account of the coal shortage our outside electrical supply will be cut off to-morrow.

We are short of fuel ourselves. It is my opinion that we will be compelled to shut down in a day or two for an indefinite period. I guess this puts an end to our conference. There's not much use of us to sit here and plan how to give away ten million dollars with an indefinite shutdown confronting us."

" All the more reason why we should go on with our work," was Edsel's answer, " for if there is a prospect of closing down the plant, the men will only need the bonus all the more."

Illustrations could be multiplied indefinitely of the ability, courage, justice and generosity of the House of Ford as it is represented in the second generation. I know of no man who has come in contact with Edsel Ford who does not have for him a real affection and admiration. He is the kind of man that men want to see succeed, for there is in him the kind of spirit that guides private wealth in channels that makes for social and industrial betterment.

# CHAPTER XIX

## THE SON AND HIS FATHER'S SHOES

WHAT will become of the House of Ford when its founder passes out? Will the son be able to fill his father's shoes?

The sons of the creators of vast fortunes and the builders of colossal industries do not always inherit the mental equipment and develop the moral character necessary to the conduct of the business established by their fathers. Fortunes tend to self-destruction by destroying those who inherit them. Great wealth is frequently dissipated in the second and third generations. A great industry often begins to disintegrate with the death of its founder, unless he is wise enough to provide that strangers shall take over its management for the benefit of his heirs.

In some instances the son does inherit the ability of his father. Two notable examples of

this are to be found in the House of Morgan
and the House of Rockefeller, and I feel quite
safe in predicting that Edsel Ford will take
his place along with the younger Morgan and
Rockefeller as an able successor to a gifted
father.

The House of Ford has nothing to fear in
the second generation. The son of Henry
Ford is well equipped, both as to character
and ability, for the management of the
colossal industry that will ultimately come
under his control. I do not mean to say that
the shoes of the father will prove an exact fit
for the son. They may prove a little oversize
in length, meaning by that that the son's stride
may not be quite so long, quite so swift and
daring, but a little more deliberate, a little
more conservative, than the stride of the father.
And I would not be surprised if the son should
find the father's shoes a little undersize in
width, meaning by that that the son has more
of a reasoned than an intuitive method of arriving at conclusions; that I credit him with
an intellectual breadth and balance, with a
sympathy and tolerance of mind, an under-

standing heart, a less ruthless manner of putting down his foot, than I credit to the father. The son is a composite in whom is to be found much of the father's ability, broad humanitarian impulses, together with certain elements of strength inherited from his mother to whom Mr. Ford attributes, and justly so, much of his success. So it may be that slight alterations may have to be made in the father's shoes in order to make them a comfortable fit for the son, but what is lost in length will be gained in breadth, and the area of the sole in contact with the ground will be no less in the second generation than in the first. I can see no reason to fear that the House of Ford will suffer at the hands of the son.

# INDEX

# INDEX

# INDEX

# INDEX

# INDEX

196

# INDEX

gambler, 33; author runs foot race with, 33; generosity to employees, 34; and profit-sharing, 34, 35; and labor, 35; tastes and habits, 36; his idea of wealth, 36, 39, 40; love of home life, 36, 37; builds first house, 36; his idea of a home, 37; his new home on the Rouge, 37, 38; his gospel of work, 38; some elements of his success, 41-48; his most valuable contribution to humanity, 41; temperamental and erratic, 42; prominent but not eminent, 42; lacks traits of true greatness, 42, 43; his opportunity to achieve an enviable reputation, 43; lack of sustained interest, 43, 44; enthusiasm in new enterprise in social justice, 44; his success no mere accident, 44, 45; and standardization, 45; idea of automobile manufacture for the masses, 45, 46; his courage and tenacity, 46; dislike for quarrels but a good fighter, 47; of Irish descent, 47; loves a lawsuit, 47; and the Selden patent trial, 47; the Dodge and *Tribune* trials, 47; the Newberry contest, 47; never forgets, 47, 48; mental traits and characteristics of, 48-57; a cross section of his mind, 49; complexes, 49; a supernormal perception in certain lines, 49; how his mind acts, 50; his belief in first impulses, 50, 51; has courage of his convictions, 51; and his executives, 52,

53; feeling toward college trained men, 53-55; realization of his limitations would have helped, 54; his mistakes in entering certain fields of endeavor, 55; not an illiterate man, 56; and "The Greatest Thing in the World," 56; his estimate of Emerson, 56; and the law of compensation, 56, 57; his birth, 58; impression made on a well-known writer by, 58; his love for children and youth, 58, 59; love for the birds and animals, 59, 63; his most intimate counselors, 63; friendship with Burroughs and Edison, 63-69; and a special trip with Edison, 65-69; a farmer's opinion of the Ford car, 65, 66; an affable and democratic man, 70; of generous impulses, 70; how he handles some requests, 70, 71; difficult of access, 71, 72; no desire for social distinction, 72, 73; the Chinese Wall around, 73; not a good mixer, 74; his aloofness, 74; importunate demands for help on, 74-76; so-called interviews with, 76, 77; his manner of talking, 77, 78; the isolation of his mind, 78, 79; the church and, 80-92; a special sermon for, 80-85; his idea of costly church buildings, 82; contributions to social activities of the church, 85; not a churchman, 90; and Dives, Lazarus and others, 93-103; and beggars, 94-97; his treatment of new

197

# INDEX

# INDEX

# INDEX

# INDEX

# INDEX

# INDEX

# INDEX